500

barbecue sizzlers

500

barbecue sizzlers

Paul Kirk

APPLE

A Quintet Book

First published in the UK in 2008 by
Apple Press
7 Greenland Street
London NW1 0ND
United Kingdom

ISBN: 978-1-84543-251-5
QTT.BQS

This book was conceived, designed, and produced by
Quintet Publishing Limited
6 Blundell Street
London N7 9BH
United Kingdom

Managing Editor: Donna Gregory
Editorial Assistant: Robert Davies
Designer: Dean Martin
Art Director: Sofia Henry
Photography: Ian Garlick
Food Stylist: Judith Fertig
Publisher: Gillian Laskier

10 9 8 7 6 5 4 3 2 1

Manufactured in Singapore by Pica Digital Pte Ltd.
Printed in China by SNP Leefung Printers Ltd.

contents

getting fired up

Grilling means cooking food directly over a heat source, sealing the food on the outside with a beautifully charred crust while the inside remains tender and juicy. Strictly speaking, barbecuing refers to cooking over indirect heat, under a cover, allowing heat to be conducted around the food as in an oven. Nowadays people use the terms grilling and barbecuing interchangeably, and this book goes along with the trend, taking care to specify when the indirect, covered method of cooking is intended.

choosing your barbecue grill

Choosing a barbecue can be a difficult decision as so many cooking vessels are included under that term, from a hole in the ground to an elaborate structure that serves effectively as an outdoor kitchen. The most widely available options are explained below so that you can choose wisely.

Charcoal barbecues are said by purists to be the only option. They claim that charcoal is the only way to achieve a genuine smoky flavour in the barbecued food; and they believe the act of stoking and tending a fire to be basic to the age-old experience of outdoor grilling. Operating a charcoal barbecue, though, requires more skill than electric or gas versions. **Gas barbecues** are easier to control than charcoal barbecues and can be made ready for use almost immediately. The lava rocks or flavouring plates that cook the food are heated by propane or natural gas. They are an excellent choice for a barbecue that is going to be used frequently.
Electric barbecues are available in small portable forms or as large trolley barbecues. They provide a good constant heat source but cannot reach the high temperatures of charcoal. They must be used close to a power source or with a long extension cord.

the right fuel for charcoal barbecues

Lumpwood charcoal burns hotter and cleaner than charcoal briquettes. It ignites quickly and burns well for about 45 minutes, perfect for searing food quickly.

Briquette charcoal is made from compressed charcoal particles that are impregnated with chemicals to help it ignite more easily. It burns for longer than natural charcoal and provides a steady heat source.

Wood can be used in the form of logs, chunks or chips. Don't use resinous soft woods such as pine. A handful of wood chips thrown onto hot coals will impart different flavours to your grill – try cherry wood for a slightly sweet smoke; mesquite for strong, earthy flavours; or hickory for a pungently smoky taste.

lighting up

Your barbecue should be sited on solid, level ground away from low trees. Clean and oil it before use, and always preheat it so that it reaches the desired temperature before you begin to cook. When lighting up, make sure you are dressed sensibly; use oven gloves and a protective apron, and keep children and animals away. Never light up in a high wind and keep matches and lighter fuels a safe distance away from the flame. In the event of a flare-up, use your spray bottle of water or a handful of bicarbonate of soda to douse the flames.

maintaining your barbecue

Each time you are preparing to barbecue, check that the connecting hoses and taps are in good order on a gas barbecue. Periodically check the wires and circuits on an electric barbecue. Oil your barbecue regularly so that food does not stick. Keep the rack grease-free by scrubbing with a wire brush after cooking. When the ashes have cooled, clean them from your firebox and dispose of them in a metal rubbish bin.

best cuts for the barbecue

poultry and game

Whole birds and juicy cuts – such as thighs and wings – are the best choices. A large, whole bird will not cook on an open barbecue unless it is split or jointed. However, it can be spit-roasted if you have this facility. Always pierce the bird between the thigh and breast – when the liquid runs clear, the bird is cooked. Split a bird by placing it on its back and cutting through either side of the backbone, removing it completely. Turn the bird over and flatten with the heel of your hand. Jointing will provide two breasts, thighs, drumsticks and wings.

lamb

Loin and sirloin chops, steaks from the leg and fillets are all good cuts for barbecuing. To prepare chops, trim all but a thin layer of fat from the outside and any other excess fat. This will help minimise flare-ups. Kebabs are best made from a shoulder joint. Meat from the leg is leaner. Minced lamb can be made from shoulder or cheaper cuts. Put the meat through the mincer two or three times at least to ensure a smooth texture.

pork

Pork tends to be a little tougher than beef or lamb. Because it needs to be well cooked, there is a danger that it may dry out; it will therefore benefit greatly from being marinated. Spareribs, chops, and tenderloin are all suitable for barbecuing, as is minced pork. To prepare, trim all but a 1 cm ($^1/_2$ in) layer of fat from the outside of chops, and any other visible excess fat. Spareribs benefit from long, slow cooking, and may be precooked in an oven, leaving the last 15 minutes of cooking to be carried out on a barbecue.

beef

Choose the best quality meat that you can afford. Rump, sirloin, fillet, T-bone and rib eye steak are the most tender cuts and best able to withstand high heat without becoming tough. Look for lean meat with a fine marbling of fat, which will keep the meat moist during cooking. To prepare beef, trim the fat to a thickness of 1 cm ($\frac{1}{2}$ in). This will minimise flare-ups but leave sufficient fat to keep the meat moist. With the point of a sharp knife, cut through the sinew and remaining fat around the edge at 2.5 cm (1 in) intervals to avoid curling during cooking.

fish

The range of fish and shellfish available for barbecuing is enormous. Whether the fish is large or small, whole or filleted, it will cook to a delicate and delicious flakiness. Oily fish such as salmon and mackerel are an excellent choice. To keep the fish moist, marinate it first and brush it frequently with oil during cooking. Fish can also be wrapped in vine leaves, lettuce or bacon to help prevent it from drying out. It can also be cooked in heavy-duty kitchen foil parcels, although it will lose the smoky flavour done this way. If you are making kebabs, use only firm fish such as monkfish or salmon.

temperatures

Cooking times depend on the heat of the barbecue and the thickness of the food being cooked. As a rough guide to temperature, the fire is hot if you can only bear to hold your hand 15 cm (6 in) above the grill rack for just two seconds. This is suitable for searing. The fire is medium-hot if you can hold your hand over the heat at the same height for four seconds, and low if you can hold your hand there for more than six seconds.

approximate cooking times

170 g (6 oz) boneless chicken breast	7 to 8 minutes on each side
170 g (6 oz) boneless chicken thigh	4 to 5 minutes on each side
225 g (8 oz) chicken drumstick	15 to 20 minutes, turning often
255 g (9 oz) chicken quarter	25 to 30 minutes, turning often
760 g (1 lb 11 oz) chicken half	35 to 40 minutes, turning often
Chicken wing	20 to 25 minutes, turning often
Chicken liver	15 to 20 minutes, turning often
Boneless duck breast	10 minutes on each side
Turkey breast	10 to 12 minutes on each side
225 g to 250 g (7 to 9 oz) fish steak	4 to 5 minutes on each side
Small fish, up to 280 g (10 oz)	6 to 7 minutes on each side
1.35 kg (3 lb 6 oz) whole fish	12 to 15 minutes on each side
Kebab, 2.5 cm (1 in) cubes of fish	7 to 8 minutes on each side
Large prawn, unshelled	2 to 3 minutes on each side
Courgette or aubergine, 2 cm- ($^3/_4$ in-) thick slices	6 to 8 minutes, turning once
Potato or sweet potato, 140 g (5 oz) pieces	30 minutes, turning once
Tomato, halved	10 to 15 minutes
Mushroom cap	4 minutes
Onion, whole	45 to 50 minutes
2.5 cm (1 in) thick lamb chop	8 to 10 minutes on each side
170 g (6 oz) lamb fillet	4 to 5 minutes on each side
4 cm- ($1^1/_2$ in-) thick lamb leg steak	6 to 7 minutes on each side
Lamb or pork kebab	10 to 15 minutes, turning often
2.5 cm- (1 in-) thick pork chop	8 to 10 minutes on each side
450 g (1 lb) pork tenderloin	25 minutes, turning often

Single pork ribs	1 hour, turning often
Rump or sirloin steak, medium well done	5 to 6 minutes on each side
Fillet steak, medium well done	7 to 8 minutes on each side
2.5 cm- (1 in-) thick burger, medium well done	5 minutes on each side

smoking

Smoking is a way of preparing meat or fish by exposing it to the aromatic smoke of burning hardwood after it has been salted or pickled for a time in brine. Traditionally this method was used to keep food edible for long periods; nowadays it is principally used to add flavour. Home smoking is easy: you can make a smoker out of any barbecue which has a cover, so long as the temperature is controllable. You must be able to adjust the airflow to the heat source, which will control the heat of the fire (with less oxygen the fire will burn more slowly), and you need to be able to regulate the escaping air as this affects how much smoke will be kept in the food chamber. Hardwood is the classic smoldering agent and you could experiment widely with different types of wood and the scents of their smoke.

setting up your smoker

You need wood chips for flavour as well as charcoal for heat. I also suggest you use a water pan, which will keep the atmosphere in the smoker humid and help retain moisture in the food. Place your hot coals over an air vent if possible; this will allow you to control the heat by allowing air into and out of the smoker. Place the water pan up against the hot coals. Place the meat on the smoker and place the lid on top, with the vent holes opposite the hot coals. Cook until ready. If you are smoking for more than about an hour, replenish the coals with hot ones as needed.

marinades and rubs

The basic items in any barbecue cook's repertoire are the seasonings that can be applied to a joint of meat, piece of fish or array of vegetables a few hours in advance, allowing their flavours to soak into the food.

garlic-herb butter

Try this melted over simply grilled fish or asparagus.

225 g (8 oz) butter, softened
60 ml (2 fl oz) vegetable oil
60 ml (2 fl oz) buttermilk
1 tbsp torn fresh basil leaves

1 tbsp fresh oregano leaves
12 cloves garlic, pressed
1 tsp sea salt
$1/8$ tsp cayenne pepper

Combine all the ingredients and blend well. Form into logs and wrap in cling film. Chill in a refrigerator and slice as needed. Vary the taste by adding 225 g (8 oz) grated cheddar cheese to make a garlic-cheese butter, or roasting the garlic for 45 minutes in a hot oven before peeling the cloves and mashing them into the butter.

basic barbecue rub

Rub this into steaks or chops before cooking for a classic barbecue flavour.

50 g (2 oz) granulated sugar
1 tbsp seasoned salt
1 tbsp garlic salt
1 tbsp onion salt
1 tbsp celery salt
2 tbsp sweet paprika

1 tbsp chilli powder
1 tbsp freshly ground black pepper
$1/2$ tsp ground ginger
$1/2$ tsp ground allspice
$1/2$ tsp dry mustard
$1/4$ tsp cayenne pepper

Stir all the ingredients together and blend well. Store in an airtight container in a cool, dark place. You can create your own barbecue rubs using this formula, making sure to get a balance between sugar and salt, always to use paprika for colour, and to add up to a teaspoon of each of your three favorite seasonings. If you want heat, add up to a teaspoon of the chilli-based seasoning you prefer.

tomato barbecue sauce

Barbecue sauces need a base – tomato, vinegar or mustard – as well as both a sweet and sour element, and the spices and seasonings of your choice. This one is a winner. Throughout this book, where recipes call simply for barbecue sauce, use either the recipe below or a good shop-bought version.

500 ml (18 fl oz) tomato ketchup
115 g (4 oz) dark brown sugar
60 ml (2 fl oz) white wine vinegar
2 tbsp Worcestershire sauce
1 tsp liquid smoke
1 tbsp chilli powder

1 tsp finely ground black pepper
2 tsp salt
1 tsp ground allspice
1 tsp garlic granules
1 tsp dry mustard
$^{1}/_{4}$ tsp chipotle powder (optional)

Combine all the dry ingredients in a saucepan. Add the liquid ingredients, except the ketchup. Stir well until all are incorporated. Stir in the ketchup and blend in. Bring the mixture slowly to the boil, reduce the heat and simmer gently for 20 minutes, stirring occasionally. (Be careful when boiling ketchup as it pops and spits.) Leave to cool. Store in the refrigerator until ready to use.

sizzling appetisers

Barbecues are perfect for bite-size appetisers, ideal
for getting the mouth watering before the main
event! Prepare some enticing treats on the barbecue
to offer when your guests arrive – perhaps some
grilled quesadillas or buffalo wings with hot pepper
sauce, grilled oysters, or skewered prawns with
sweet chilli sauce.

cheese-stuffed mushrooms

see variations page 34

Tasty stuffed mushrooms are always a favourite party appetiser. This recipe is perfect for any occasion.

24 medium mushrooms
450 g (1 lb) spiced sausage
225 g (8 oz) cream cheese

55 g (2 oz) Cheddar cheese, grated
1 to 2 tsp crushed dried chillies
2 tbsp freshly grated Parmesan cheese

Wash the mushrooms, remove the stems and pat the caps dry with kitchen paper. Preheat the barbecue to 120°C (250°F).

Cook the sausage in a large frying pan until done, drain and place in a mixing bowl. Add the cream cheese, Cheddar cheese and crushed chillies. Mix well. Place 1 heaped teaspoon of the mixture into each mushroom cap. Place the stuffed mushroom caps on a shallow baking tin that will fit into your barbecue and sprinkle with Parmesan.

Prepare a covered barbecue for smoking (see page 11) and smoke-roast the mushrooms, covered, for 30 to 45 minutes. Remove and allow to cool for 5 minutes. Arrange the stuffed mushrooms on a decorative serving platter and serve hot.

Serves 8

barbecued wings

see variations page 35

Sticky barbecued chicken wings are a perennial favourite and a great snack to offer before the main event. You can't make too many – they will disappear as fast as you can make them!

2 tsp coarse sea salt
1 tsp freshly ground black pepper
1 tsp paprika
1 tsp chilli powder

$^1/_2$ tsp ground celery seeds
1.35 kg (3 lbs) chicken wings, tips removed
355 ml (12 fl oz) barbecue sauce

Combine the salt, pepper, paprika, chilli powder and celery seeds. Blend well. Roll the wings in this mixture. Barbecue over a medium heat directly or with indirect heat, covered. Turn the wings about every 10 minutes for 30 minutes to 1 hour, depending on how hot you are cooking them.

When the wings are done, place in a large bowl and pour the sauce over them. Toss to coat the wings with the sauce. Serve hot.

Serves 6–8

charcoal-grilled skewered prawns

see variations page 36

Quickly barbecued prawns retain their natural sweetness and sea-fresh flavour.

900 g (2 lbs) large prawns in the shell
   (20 to 25 in number)
5 tbsp vegetable oil
120 ml (4 fl oz) fresh lime juice
3 tbsp dry white wine or vermouth
1 clove garlic, crushed

1 tbsp finely chopped shallots or spring onions
   (white part only)
1 tsp sea salt
$1\frac{1}{2}$ tsp chopped fresh dill or $\frac{1}{2}$ tsp dried
Several dashes chilli sauce

Place the prawns in a shallow ceramic or glass baking dish. Combine the remaining ingredients and pour over the prawns. Cover and chill for several hours or overnight. Drain the prawns and reserve the marinade.

Thread the prawns onto skewers or place in a wire grill basket. Preheat the barbecue, then grill the prawns over hot coals, turning and brushing with the reserved marinade, until pink and cooked through, about 4 to 5 minutes. Serve on small wooden skewers.

Makes 30 servings

grilled oysters san felipe

see variations page 37

This spicy sauce is the perfect foil for fresh oysters cooked in the half-shell.

20 oysters in shells
for the sauce
2 tbsp finely chopped onion
1 tbsp unsalted butter
2 tbsp plain flour
120 ml (4 fl oz) fish stock
120 ml (4 fl oz) flat beer
2 tsp Tabasco sauce

2 tbsp freshly grated Parmesan cheese
for the crumb topping
28 g (1 oz) fine dry breadcrumbs
28 g (1 oz) freshly grated Parmesan cheese
2 tbsp unsalted butter, melted
1 tbsp chopped fresh coriander
1 tsp Tabasco sauce

Clean, open and shuck the oysters. Place them in their rinsed and dried bottom shell halves. In a small saucepan cook the onion in 1 tablespoon butter until soft. Stir in the flour; add the stock, beer and 2 teaspoons Tabasco. Cook and stir until thickened and bubbly. Remove from the heat and stir in 2 tablespoons cheese.

To make the crumb topping, combine the breadcrumbs, 35 g (1$^{1}/_{4}$ oz) cheese, melted butter, coriander and 1 teaspoon Tabasco. Spoon a tablespoon of sauce over each oyster and sprinkle 1 teaspoon of the crumb mixture on top. Line a shallow baking tin with rock salt to a depth of 1.5 cm ($^{1}/_{2}$ in) (or use crumpled foil to prevent the shells from tipping), creating dips to cradle the shell halves. Cook the oysters over a medium heat for 8 to 10 minutes or until heated through.

Serves 10

bacon wraps

see variations page 38

The soft meatiness of these simple wraps is lifted by the crunch of the water chestnut.

225 g (8 oz) tin water chestnuts, drained
455 g (1 lb) streaky bacon rashers, cut in half
225 g (8 oz) chicken livers, cut in pieces

Water-soaked cocktail sticks
28 g (1 oz) soy sauce
55 g (2 oz) loosely packed light brown sugar

Place a water chestnut on a halved bacon rasher and top with a piece of chicken liver. Wrap the bacon over the top of the liver and secure with a cocktail stick. (Roll or screw in the cocktail stick to avoid breaking water chestnuts.)

Repeat until you fill a baking dish in a single layer. Mix the soy sauce and brown sugar, and sprinkle over the top of the bacon wraps.

Grill the bacon wraps over a medium heat, covered, turning occasionally. Cook for about 8 to 10 minutes, or until the bacon is crisp and browned. Serve with cocktail sticks.

Serves 8

bbq sweet and spicy meatballs

see variations page 39

These richly flavoured meatballs make a tempting informal appetiser. If you're handing them out with drinks, serve them with cocktail sticks. If you're serving them at the table, serve chunks of bread for mopping up the luscious sauce.

680 g (1¹/₂ lbs) minced beef
50 g (2 oz) fresh breadcrumbs
120 ml (4 fl oz) milk
1 large egg, lightly beaten
1 tbsp Worcestershire sauce
35 g (1¹/₄ oz) freshly grated Parmesan cheese
2 tsp sea salt
1 tsp freshly ground black pepper

1 tbsp garlic granules
1 tbsp onion granules
2 tsp dried oregano
2 tsp dried basil
for the sauce
575 ml (1 pint) barbecue sauce
235 ml (8 oz) seedless raspberry jam
1 tsp chilli powder

Preheat a smoker or barbecue to between 110˚C and 120˚C (230˚F and 250˚F). Line a shallow baking tin with foil. Set aside. Combine the minced beef, breadcrumbs, milk, egg, Worcestershire sauce, cheese, salt, pepper, garlic, onion granules, oregano and basil. Form into 2.5 cm (1 in) meatballs and place on the foil-lined baking tin so they are not touching each other. Barbecue over indirect heat for 45 minutes to 1 hour or until cooked through.

While the meatballs are grilling, bring the barbecue sauce, raspberry jam and chilli powder to a simmer, stirring until well combined. Toss the cooked meatballs with the raspberry sauce until well coated. Serve hot.

Makes approximately 50 meatballs

grilled pizza

see variations page 40

You can use pitta bread or tortillas for the pizza crust instead of this straightforward homemade bread dough.

1 1/2 tsp dried yeast
235 ml (8 fl oz) lukewarm water
1/2 tsp sugar
340 g (12 oz) plain flour
3 tbsp olive oil

60 ml (2 fl oz) tomato sauce
170 g (6 oz) sliced pepperoni
1 red pepper, roasted, skinned and sliced
75 g (3 oz) stoned and sliced black olives
225 g (8 oz) mozzarella cheese

Combine the yeast, water and sugar together and allow to stand in a warm place until the mixture starts to foam. Add the yeast mixture to the flour and oil, and combine to form a dough. Knead on a lightly floured surface until smooth and elastic.

Cover and leave to stand in a warm place until doubled in size. Meanwhile, lightly oil a baking sheet. Punch down the dough and roll out to a rectangle the size of the baking sheet, and place onto the sheet.

Spread the dough with the tomato sauce and top with pepperoni, red peppers, olives and cheese. Cook the pizza indirectly on high heat, covered, for approximately 20 minutes. Place the baking sheet directly over one burner on high for about 2 minutes to crisp the base.

Serves 6–8

grilled quesadillas

see variations page 41

This Mexican staple is ideal served with salsa, guacamole or a black-bean dip.

4 flour tortillas, 25 cm (10-in) diameter   **Freshly ground black pepper**
115 g (4 oz) Cheddar cheese, grated

Prepare a charcoal barbecue or preheat a gas barbecue for direct barbecuing over medium heat.

Lay the tortillas on a flat work surface. Sprinkle half of each tortilla with a quarter of the cheese and some pepper. You can add other fillings if you like; divide them among the tortillas, distributing them evenly over the cheese. Fold the empty half of the tortilla over the filled portion.

The tortillas are not sealed, so you need to be careful when you transfer them to the barbecue – use a wide fish slice to do so. Grill for about 5 minutes in total, turning over once (carefully) halfway through the cooking time. Cut each quesadilla into 4 wedges before serving.

Serves 4

tomato-basil bruschetta

see variations page 42

A popular Italian classic, this is both simple to prepare and a joy to eat!

4 or 5 medium, ripe tomatoes, peeled and
   coarsely chopped
75 ml (2$^1/_2$ fl oz) olive oil
3 tbsp balsamic vinegar
2 tbsp chopped fresh basil or $^1/_2$ tsp dried

Pinch of freshly ground black pepper
1 long baguette or 1 ciabatta loaf, cut into
   1.5 cm ($^1/_2$-in) thick slices
4 cloves garlic, sliced in half
Freshly grated Parmesan cheese, if desired

Drain the tomatoes in a sieve for 20 minutes. Combine the oil, vinegar, basil and pepper in a large bowl and whisk together. Add the drained tomatoes to the dressing and toss to coat. Leave to marinate for at least 15 minutes, or up to 30 minutes.

Toast the bread slices on both sides on a medium-hot grill. When toasted, rub the cut side of the garlic on the top of each slice. Top each slice with some of the tomato mixture. You may serve this now or, if desired, sprinkle with Parmesan cheese and return to the grill, covered, until it melts. (It doesn't take long.)

Makes 10–12 slices

thai chicken satay skewers

see variations page 43

Creamy peanut sauce with tender skewered chicken is a deservedly popular Thai classic.

455 g (1 lb) boneless, skinless chicken breasts
for the marinade
75 ml (2½ fl oz) soy sauce
2 tbsp fresh lime juice
2 cloves garlic, pressed
2 tsp grated fresh ginger
1 tsp crushed dried chillies

2 tbsp water
for the peanut sauce
175 ml (6 fl oz) unsweetened coconut milk
1 tbsp smooth peanut butter
4 spring onions with tops cut into 2.5 cm (1 in) pieces
36 water-soaked bamboo skewers

Cut the chicken into 5mm (¼ in) wide strips; place in a shallow dish. Combine the soy sauce, lime juice, garlic, ginger and crushed chillies in a bowl. Set aside 3 tablespoons of the mixture; cover and refrigerate. Add the water to the remaining mixture. Pour over the chicken and toss to coat. Cover the chicken and marinate in the refrigerator for between 30 minutes and 2 hours, stirring occasionally.

Preheat a grill to medium. Meanwhile, combine the coconut milk, reserved marinade and peanut butter in small saucepan. Bring to the boil over a medium-high heat, stirring constantly. Reduce the heat and simmer for 2 to 4 minutes, until the sauce thickens. Keep warm. Drain the chicken and discard the marinade. Weave 3 to 4 chicken strips accordion-style onto each skewer, alternating with spring onion pieces. Grill the skewers on the uncovered grill for 6 to 8 minutes or until the chicken is cooked. Turn halfway through the grilling time. Serve with warm peanut sauce for dipping.

Makes 36 skewers

marinated grilled artichokes

see variations page 44

Grilling artichokes is the perfect way to prepare them, as they maintain a firm texture. Their unique flavour is enhanced by the simple marinade.

4 large globe artichokes
60 ml (2 fl oz) balsamic vinegar
60 ml (2 fl oz) water

60 ml (2 fl oz) soy sauce
1 tbsp grated fresh ginger
60 ml (2 fl oz) olive oil

Trim the stems off the artichokes, leaving about 5 cm (2 in) of stem on each artichoke. Cut off the sharp point on each leaf. Boil or steam the artichokes until the bases pierce easily, or a leaf pulls off easily. Drain the artichokes and cool. Cut each artichoke in half lengthways and scrape out the hairy centre and any purple-tipped leaves.

Mix the remaining ingredients in a large polythene bag. Place the artichokes in the bag and coat all sides of the artichokes. Marinate for at least 1 hour, but for the best flavour marinate overnight in the refrigerator.

Drain the artichokes, reserving the marinade. Place them cut side down on a rack over a medium heat. Grill for 5 to 7 minutes, until lightly browned on the cut side. Turn them over and drizzle some of the remaining marinade over them. Grill for 3 to 4 minutes more, until the leaf tips are lightly charred. Serve hot or at room temperature.

Makes 8 servings

bacon-wrapped jalapeño peppers

see variations page 45

These spicy stuffed chillies are easy to prepare in advance, as you can chill or freeze them before cooking. Increase the quantities to suit; you can never have too many!

25 fresh jalapeño peppers
455 g (1 lb) cream cheese, softened
225 g (8 oz) grated Cheddar cheese

900 g (2 lb) bacon
55 g (2 oz) dark brown sugar
Water-soaked cocktail sticks

Use hot or mild jalapeño peppers, according to your preference. Cut the tops off the jalapeños. Remove the veins and seeds.

Combine the cheeses and blend until they are soft enough to pipe through a piping bag. Fill the jalapeños. Slice the bacon rashers in half and coat with the dark brown sugar. Wrap the bacon around the jalapeños, covering the opened end, and secure with a cocktail stick.

Stand the peppers upright together in an aluminum baking tin so the cheese won't come out. Preheat a smoker or barbecue to 110˚C to 120˚C (230˚F to 250˚F) and smoke the peppers for about 1 hour, or until the bacon is cooked.

Makes 25

variations

cheese-stuffed mushrooms

see base recipe page 15

crab-stuffed mushrooms
Replace the stuffing with a crab meat stuffing. Sauté 1 tablespoon butter, 2 pressed cloves garlic, 4 sliced spring onions, 75 g (6 oz) drained and flaked crab meat, and 50 g (2 oz) fresh breadcrumbs. Cool and add 140 g (5 oz) chopped water chestnuts, 120 ml (4 fl oz) mayonnaise, and salt and pepper to taste.

blue cheese-stuffed mushrooms
Replace the stuffing with this mixture: sauté 225 g (8 oz) crumbled blue cheese; 2 pressed cloves garlic; 250 g (10 oz) frozen chopped spinach, thawed and drained; 55 g (2 oz) unsalted butter at room temperature; salt and pepper to taste. Cool before using.

bacon and olive-stuffed mushrooms
Replace the stuffing with a mixture of 125 g (4½ oz) freshly grated Parmesan cheese, 55 g (2 oz) chopped olives, 2 tablespoons Worcestershire sauce and 14 bacon rashers that have been cooked until crisp and crumbled.

roasted red pepper-stuffed mushrooms
Replace the stuffing with a mixture of 225 g (8 oz) softened cream cheese, 55 g (2 oz) roasted red pepper, 2 tablespoons freshly grated Parmesan cheese, 2 pressed cloves garlic and ½ teaspoon chilli powder.

barbecued wings

see base recipe page 16

grilled sweet chilli wings
Replace the barbecue sauce with a sweet chilli sauce: combine 60 ml (2 fl oz) sweet chilli sauce, 60 g (2¼ oz) melted butter, 1 tablespoon Worcestershire sauce and 1 teaspoon lemon juice.

barbecued tex-mex wings
Omit the celery seeds in the seasoning mix. Replace the barbecue sauce with a spicy Tex-Mex sauce: combine ½ teaspoon each of garlic granules, onion granules, cumin, coriander and cayenne with 1 teaspoon mesquite liquid smoke (optional) and 60 ml (2 fl oz) each of ketchup, cider vinegar, honey and brown sugar.

teriyaki wings
Replace the paprika, chilli powder and celery seeds in the seasoning mix with 2 teaspoons ground ginger and 2 teaspoons garlic granules. Replace barbecue sauce with teriyaki sauce.

spicy honey-garlic wings
Omit the chilli powder, celery seeds and barbecue sauce. Add 1 teaspoon each of ground ginger and garlic granules. For the sauce, combine 235 ml (8 fl oz) clear honey, 120 ml (4 fl oz) golden syrup, 8 large pressed cloves of garlic and 1 teaspoon crushed dried chillies. Heat the sauce gently in a frying pan and pour over the grilled wings.

variations

charcoal-grilled skewered prawns

see base recipe page 19

margarita prawn skewers
Replace the marinade with a mixture of 120 ml (4 fl oz) tequila, 4 tablespoons fresh orange juice, 2 tablespoons vegetable oil and 120 ml (4 fl oz) fresh lime juice. Alternate with the prawns on the skewers 3 fresh red chillies, cut into 1.5 cm ($\frac{1}{2}$ in) slices, and 1 large red pepper, cut into 1.5 cm ($\frac{1}{2}$ in) squares.

spicy grilled prawns
Replace the marinade with a mixture of 2 tablespoons each of olive oil, chopped garlic, Worcestershire sauce and fresh lemon juice; 6 tablespoons melted unsalted butter; 2 teaspoons each of chilli powder and freshly ground black pepper; and 1 teaspoon sea salt.

honey grilled prawns
While grilling, baste the unmarinated skewers with mixture of 120 ml (4 fl oz) each of clear honey and fresh lime juice, grated zest of 1 lime and 1 teaspoon each of sea salt and white pepper.

zesty grilled prawns
Replace the marinade with a mixture of 235 ml (8 fl oz) pineapple juice; 60 ml (2 fl oz) each of fresh lemon juice and vegetable oil; 1 tablespoon soy sauce; and 1 teaspoon each of sweet chilli sauce, celery seeds and sea salt.

variations

grilled oysters san felipe

see base recipe page 20

grilled bay oysters
Omit the crumb topping. Replace the sauce with a mixture of 2 tablespoons unsalted butter; ½ small onion, chopped; 120 ml (4 fl oz) chilli sauce; 1 tablespoon each of clear honey and Worcestershire sauce; 6 dashes Tabasco sauce. Sauté until the onion is soft, then leave to cool before topping the oysters.

hickory-smoked herb oysters
Replace the sauce with a mixture of 4 tablespoons unsalted butter, 60 ml (2 fl oz) dry sherry, 2 large pressed cloves garlic, 2 teaspoons dried basil and 25 g (1 oz) finely chopped walnuts. Sauté until the garlic is cooked, then leave to cool before topping the oysters. Replace the crumb topping with a squeeze of lemon juice over the oysters and a sprinkle of freshly grated Parmesan cheese. Use 1 bag of hickory chips for grilling.

barbecued oysters with spicy garlic butter
Omit the crumb topping. Replace the sauce with a mixture of 225 g (8 oz) unsalted butter, 2 tablespoons chopped fresh parsley, 1 tablespoon each of fresh lemon juice and pressed garlic, and 1 teaspoon each of grated lemon zest and sweet chilli sauce. Sauté until the garlic is cooked, then leave to cool before topping the oysters.

grilled oysters in the whole shell
Omit the crumb topping and sauce. Do not open the oysters. Clean them and grill until they open. Serve with Tabasco sauce.

variations

bacon wraps

see base recipe page 23

bacon-wrapped water chestnuts
Prepare the basic recipe, omitting the chicken livers, soy sauce and sugar. Combine and simmer in a saucepan 575 ml (1 pint) ketchup and 2 tablespoons Worcestershire sauce. Pour this sauce over the grilled water chestnuts.

bacon-wrapped pineapple chunks
Prepare the basic recipe, omitting the chicken livers, soy sauce and sugar, and replacing the water chestnuts with a 425 g (15 oz) can pineapple chunks, drained.

bacon-wrapped dates
Prepare the basic recipe, omitting the chicken livers, soy sauce and sugar, and replacing the water chestnuts with about 60 stoneless dates.

bacon-wrapped prawns
Prepare the basic recipe, omitting the chicken livers, soy sauce and sugar. Replace the water chestnuts with 455 g (1 lb) medium prawns, peeled and deveined (approximately 45), which have been seasoned with 2 teaspoons each of garlic granules and sea salt.

bbq sweet and spicy meatballs

see base recipe page 24

smoked Italian meatballs
Substitute mozzarella cheese for the Parmesan; replace the raspberry jam with 235 ml (8 fl oz) Italian tomato sauce.

barbecued teriyaki meatballs
Omit the cheese, oregano and basil. Replace the barbecue sauce and raspberry jam with teriyaki sauce and a pinch or two of ground ginger.

smoky cocktail meatballs
Omit the garlic, onion, oregano and basil, and replace with three 25 g (1 oz) packets of dry onion soup mix. Replace the sauce with a combination of 575 ml (1 pint) ketchup, 225 g (8 oz) light brown sugar and 60 ml (2 fl oz) Worcestershire sauce. Heat this sauce gently for 5 minutes and serve with the barbecued meatballs.

smoked redcurrant jelly meatballs
Omit the garlic, onion, oregano and basil. Replace the sauce with a combination of 355 ml (12 fl oz) chilli sauce, 355 ml (12 fl oz) redcurrant jelly and 1 tablespoon Dijon mustard. Heat this sauce gently for 5 minutes and serve with the barbecued meatballs.

variations

grilled pizza

see base recipe page 26

italian pizza with goat's cheese
Replace the mozzarella cheese and pepperoni with caramelised onions, goat's cheese warmed to room temperature and 5 tablespoons chopped fresh basil.

half-time pizzas
Add to the toppings 115 g (4 oz) cooked and crumbled Italian sausage and 4 rashers of back bacon, chopped.

barbecued chicken pizza
Replace the Italian sauce with 235 ml (8 fl oz) barbecue sauce. Omit the pepperoni and replace with 225 g (8 oz) barbecued chicken breast or cooked chicken, diced, 55 g (2 oz) chopped onion and 115 g (4 oz) canned mushroom stems and pieces.

blt pizza appetiser
Omit the Italian tomato sauce, pepperoni, peppers and olives. Spread the pizza crust with 120 ml (4 fl oz) mayonnaise and top with 8 to 10 rashers cooked bacon, cut into quarters. After grilling, garnish with a handful of torn romaine lettuce.

variations

grilled quesadillas

see base recipe page 27

spicy gourmet grilled quesadillas
Add to the filling ingredients 120 ml (4 fl oz) soured cream; 4 spring onions, white and green parts sliced thinly; 1 ripe tomato, peeled, seeded and finely diced; 1 to 2 jalapeño peppers, seeded and chopped; and 4 tablespoons chopped fresh coriander.

grilled chicken quesadillas
Omit the Cheddar cheese. Add 280 g (10 oz) diced cooked or barbecued chicken, 1 medium sliced red onion, 115 g (4 oz) grated Parmesan cheese, 4 tablespoons chopped fresh coriander leaves and 1 chopped jalapeño.

grilled ham quesadillas
Add 340 g (12 oz) chopped ham, 4 tablespoons finely sliced spring onions, 235 ml (8 fl oz) barbecue sauce, 1 tablespoon cider vinegar and 2 teaspoons basic barbecue rub (see page 12).

steak quesadillas
Add marinated grilled steak and your own fresh tomato and chilli salsa.

variations

tomato–basil bruschetta

see base recipe page 29

cheesy bruschetta
Omit the tomato-basil mixture and the Parmesan cheese. Spread the grilled garlic toast with 110 g (4 oz) softened goat's cheese or cream cheese. Garnish with 4 thinly sliced spring onions and sea salt to taste.

angel's bruschetta
Omit the tomato-basil mixture and the Parmesan cheese. Spread the grilled garlic toast with a mixture of 1 chopped medium onion, 1 pressed large clove garlic, ½ teaspoon each dried oregano and basil, 225 g (8 oz) thinly sliced mozzarella cheese and salt to taste.

bruschetta with roasted peppers
Omit the tomato-basil mixture and the Parmesan cheese. Spread the grilled garlic toast with a mixture of 2 medium roasted red peppers, diced; 2 cloves garlic, pressed; 2 anchovy fillets, diced; 1 tablespoon chopped Italian parsley; and salt and pepper to taste.

prawn bruschetta
Omit the tomato-basil mixture and the Parmesan cheese. Spread the grilled garlic toast with a mixture of 225 g (8 oz) cooked prawns, 2 tablespoons olive oil, 1 tablespoon each of balsamic vinegar and lemon juice and ¼ teaspoon each of garlic granules and black pepper.

thai chicken satay skewers

see base recipe page 30

s.k.'s malaysian pork satay
Replace the chicken with 450 g (1 lb) pork tenderloin. For the marinade, replace the soy sauce, lime juice, red pepper and water with 4 finely chopped shallots, 1 teaspoon each of ground coriander, cumin and salt; 1 tablespoon each of ground turmeric, sugar and vegetable oil.

rasa malaysian chicken satay
For the marinade, replace the soy sauce, lime juice, ginger and crushed chillies with 6 finely chopped shallots, 4 tablespoons each of vegetable oil and Kecap Manis, 2 tablespoons each of minced lemongrass and oyster sauce, 2 teaspoons ground turmeric, and 1 teaspoon each of ground coriander and chilli powder.

thai prawn satay
Replace the chicken with 450 g (1 lb) prawns. For the marinade, replace the soy sauce, lime juice, ginger, crushed chillies and water with 1 tablespoon each of palm sugar, soy sauce, white pepper, Thai chilli sauce and oyster sauce, and 1 teaspoon Thai curry powder.

ratami's lamb satay
Replace the chicken with 450 g (1 lb) boneless leg of lamb. For the marinade, replace the soy sauce, lime juice, ginger, crushed chillies and water with 1 chopped large shallot, 2 pressed cloves garlic, 2 tablespoons Kecap Manis, 2 tablespoons fresh lemon juice, 1 tablespoon granulated sugar, 1 teaspoon tamarind paste dissolved in 1 tablespoon hot water, and salt and pepper to taste.

variations

marinated grilled artichokes

see base recipe page 32

grilled artichokes with lemon yogurt
Replace the marinade with 175 ml (6 fl oz) olive oil, the juice of 2 lemons, 1 tablespoon each of finely chopped garlic and chopped fresh parsley, and salt and pepper to taste. Serve with lemon yogurt.

artichoke kebabs
Replace the marinade with 2 tablespoons fresh lemon juice, ½ teaspoon dried thyme and salt and pepper to taste. Thread the artichoke leaves onto water-soaked bamboo skewers. Serve with mayonnaise or a dipping sauce of your choice.

garlic-marinated artichokes
Replace the marinade with the grated zest of 2 lemons, 55g (2 oz) melted butter, 2 tablespoons each of dry white wine and fresh lemon juice, 2 teaspoons garlic salt, and freshly ground black pepper to taste. Serve with garlic mayonnaise.

citrus artichokes
Replace the marinade with 120 ml (4 fl oz) chicken stock; 3 tablespoons melted unsalted butter; 2 tablespoons each of walnut oil, olive oil and chopped flat-leaf parsley; 1 tablespoon each of lemon and orange juice, lemon and orange zest, and chopped garlic; and salt and pepper to taste.

bacon-wrapped jalapeño peppers

see base recipe page 33

smoked sausage-stuffed jalapeños
Omit the cheddar and brown sugar. Add 55 g (2 oz) cooked and crumbled smoked sausage;
4 spring onions, sliced thinly; 1 large clove garlic, pressed; and 1 tablespoon chopped fresh
flat-leaf parsley.

ham-stuffed jalapeños
Omit the cheeses and brown sugar. Add 175 g (6 oz) chopped ham, 115 g (4 oz) grated
Cheddar cheese, 1 tablespoon cider vinegar, and 2 teaspoons barbecue rub (see page 12).

chilli sausage-stuffed jalapeños
Omit the cheeses and brown sugar. Add 450 g (1 lb) pork sausage, cooked and crumbled;
1 tablespoon crushed dried chillies; and 1 tablespoon garlic salt.

crab-stuffed jalapeños
Omit the bacon, cheeses and brown sugar. Add 450 g (1 lb) white crab meat, 2 tablespoons
chopped red pepper, 2 tablespoons grated onion, 1 chopped large clove garlic,
1 tablespoon Dijon mustard and salt and pepper to taste.

spring onion-stuffed jalapeños
Omit the Cheddar and bacon. Add 55 g (2 oz) chopped spring onions to make a cream
cheese and spring onion stuffing.

flaming fish and shellfish

When it comes to barbecuing, there's little simpler
than a perfectly marinated piece of fish or shellfish,
popped on the grill until just cooked through.

brown sugar-cured salmon

see variations page 68

This quick-cure method enhances the natural sweetness of these succulent salmon fillets.

225 g (8 oz) light brown sugar
1 tbsp Cajun spice mix
1 tbsp coarse sea salt
1 tsp freshly ground black pepper

Six 170–225 g (6–8 oz) salmon fillets,
  skin on
8 tbsp Dijon mustard
115 g (4 oz) light brown sugar

Combine the 225 g (8 oz) brown sugar, Cajun spice mix, salt and pepper in a bowl and blend well.

Rinse the salmon under cold running water and pat dry with kitchen paper. Cover the fillets evenly on both sides with the sugar mixture. Place the fillets in a glass baking dish, cover and leave to cure in the refrigerator for 2 hours.

Prepare the barbecue and heat to 110°C (230°F). Remove the fillets from the cure. Using a pastry brush, paint the top of each fillet with mustard, place in the smoker (on a sheet of foil, for easy clean up), then top with the remaining 115 g (4 oz) brown sugar. Cook until the white protein comes to the top of the fillets, which will take about 35 to 40 minutes. Serve hot.

Serves 6

grilled herby lemon salmon

see variations page 69

A gutsy Italian-style mixture of garlic and herbs is a perfect complement to rich salmon steaks.

60 ml (2 fl oz) balsamic vinegar
60 ml (2 fl oz) olive oil
60 ml (2 fl oz) fresh lemon juice
1 large clove garlic, pressed
1 tbsp dried chives

$^1/_2$ tsp dried thyme
$^1/_8$ tsp dried rosemary
Sea salt and freshly ground black pepper to taste
Four 2.5 cm- (1 in-) thick salmon steaks

In a large bowl, combine all the ingredients except the salmon. Add the salmon steaks to the bowl; spoon the marinade over them until they are well coated. Cover and chill for at least 2 hours, turning the fish over after an hour.

Prepare a medium-hot barbecue. Remove the fish from the marinade and grill for 10 to 15 minutes, turning once halfway through cooking. Cook until the fish flakes easily with a fork.

Serves 6–8

'hot' grilled trout

see variations page 70

For this recipe you can use brook trout or any similar oily, freshwater fish.

4 tbsp fresh lemon juice
2 tbsp unsalted butter, melted
2 tbsp vegetable oil
2 tbsp chopped fresh parsley
2 tbsp sesame seeds

1 tbsp chilli sauce
1 tsp grated fresh ginger
$^{1}/_{2}$ tsp sea salt
Four 450 g (1 lb) fresh trout

In a shallow dish combine the lemon juice, butter, oil, parsley, sesame seeds, hot sauce, ginger and salt; mix well.

Pierce the skin of the fish in several places with the tines of a fork. Roll the fish in the juice mixture to coat inside and out. Cover and chill for 30 minutes to 1 hour, turning occasionally. Remove the fish from the marinade; reserve the marinade. Place the fish in a wire grill basket; brush with reserved marinade.

Prepare a medium-hot barbecue. Cook the fish for about 5 minutes. Turn it over, and cook for 5 minutes longer. The fish is done when the flesh flakes easily.

Serves 4

grilled tilapia

see variations page 71

Tilapia, which originated in Africa, has recently begun to spread worldwide, winning many cooks over with its tender, creamy flesh.

175 ml (6 fl oz) mayonnaise
1 tsp brown sauce
1 tsp fresh lime juice
1 tsp grated lime zest

2 tbsp freshly grated Parmesan cheese
$1/8$ tsp chopped fresh dill
4 large tilapia fillets

Mix together the mayonnaise, brown sauce, lime juice, lime zest, cheese and dill. Spread generously on both sides of the tilapia fillets.

Preheat the barbecue to medium. Place the coated fish on a preheated medium grill and cook for 3–5 minutes on each side or until the fish flakes easily with a fork.

Serves 4

grilled swordfish steaks with citrus salsa

see variations page 72

A vibrant Mexican-inspired salsa is a perfect accompaniment to meaty swordfish steaks.

235 ml (8 fl oz) chunky tomato salsa
1 tsp grated orange zest
2 tbsp fresh orange juice
1 tbsp chopped fresh coriander

1 large orange, peeled and chopped
1 medium tomato, diced
2 spring onions, thinly sliced
4 swordfish steaks, 2.5 cm (1 in) thick

Mix together the tomato salsa, orange zest, orange juice and coriander. Set aside 120 ml (4 fl oz). Add orange, tomato and onions to remaining mixture to make the citrus salsa.

Prepare the barbecue to medium-hot. Grill the fish over medium heat for 10 minutes or until done, turning once, and brushing often with the reserved salsa mixture. Serve the fish with the citrus salsa.

Serves 4

grilled halibut with pineapple

see variations page 73

Here is more proof that citrus and fish are the perfect marriage of flavours.

1 tbsp grated lime zest
2 tbsp fresh lime juice
2 tbsp light brown sugar
2 tbsp grated fresh ginger
1 tsp sea salt

$^1/_4$ tsp mild chilli powder
Four 175 g (6 oz) halibut fillets
$^1/_2$ medium pineapple, peeled and cut
    lengthways into 1.5 cm- (2 in-) thick spears

Prepare the barbecue. Place the zest, lime juice, 1 tablespoon brown sugar, 1 tablespoon ginger, salt and chilli powder in a resealable plastic bag; shake to combine. Add the fish to this bag. Reseal, shake again, place the bag on a plate and marinate at room temperature for 20 minutes, turning once.

Meanwhile, place the remaining brown sugar, ginger and pineapple in a second plastic bag. Allow to marinate for 5 minutes; remove the pineapple and add any juices to the fish bag.

Barbecue the pineapple until heated through, turning once. Remove to a serving platter and cover with foil to keep warm. Remove the fish from its marinade. Barbecue the fish over direct heat until cooked through; allow 3 to 4 minutes per side. Serve hot, with the barbecued pineapple.

Serves 4

grilled shark to die for

see variations page 74

Shark steaks are delicious and widely available, but swordfish or even tuna steaks would be just as good in this recipe.

120 ml (4 fl oz) soy sauce
120 ml (4 fl oz) fresh orange juice
60 ml (2 fl oz) ketchup
4 tbsp chopped fresh parsley

2 tbsp fresh lemon juice
1 tsp freshly ground black pepper
2 large cloves garlic, pressed
Six 175 g (6 oz) shark steaks

In a bowl, mix together the soy sauce, orange juice, ketchup, chopped parsley, lemon juice, pepper and garlic. Set aside 60 ml (2 fl oz). Add the fish; cover and marinate in the refrigerator for 2 hours.

Prepare the barbecue. Remove the fish from its marinade. Barbecue the fish over a high heat, basting frequently with the reserved marinade, for 6 minutes on each side or until the fish flakes easily when tested with a fork.

Serves 6

mexican grilled red snapper

see variations page 75

Achiote paste is a traditional Mexican ingredient with a salty, spicy flavour. You should be able to find it in specialist food shops – or make your own (see below).

120 ml (4 fl oz) achiote paste
120 ml (4 fl oz) orange juice
3 tbsp fresh lemon juice
3 tbsp fresh lime juice

Grated zest of 1 lemon and 1 lime
1 whole red snapper, gutted (about 900 g
    [2 lbs])
Heated tomato salsa

Mix the achiote paste with the citrus juices and zest. Cover all surfaces of the fish with the mixture. Place the fish in the refrigerator and leave to marinate for 30 minutes to 1 hour.

Place the fish on a barbecue preheated to medium, skin-side down. When the fish is about half done (after about 5 minutes), turn it and continue cooking for another 3 minutes. You should be able to lift the central bone out easily when the fish is cooked. Serve with heated salsa.

To make your own achiote paste, mix together 2 tablespoons ground annatto seeds or paprika, 1 tablespoon olive oil, 1 tablespoon chilli powder, 2 tablespoons chopped fresh garlic, 1 teaspoon ground allspice, $1/2$ teaspoon ground cinnamon, 2 teaspoons clear honey, 2 teaspoons dried oregano and 1 teaspoon salt. Stir in 4 tablespoons fresh orange juice to make a smooth paste.

Serves 4–6

grilled citrus tuna

see variations page 76

Tuna steaks can become tough if not cooked carefully. Tenderise them in acidic fruit juices first, then cook them briefly to retain their melting texture.

235 ml (8 fl oz) orange juice
235 ml (8 fl oz) grapefruit juice
4 tbsp lime juice
120 ml (4 fl oz) dry sherry

1 tsp dried thyme
$1/4$ tsp cayenne pepper
$1/4$ tsp sea salt
4 large tuna steaks
1 tbsp paprika

Mix the juices, sherry, thyme, cayenne pepper and salt in a shallow baking dish. Add the fish and leave to marinate for 30 minutes to 1 hour in the refrigerator. Remove the tuna from the marinade and discard the marinade. Place the fish on a barbecue preheated to high and sprinkle with paprika.

Turn the tuna after about 3 to 5 minutes and continue cooking for another 3 to 5 minutes. Allow more time if you like your fish well cooked.

Serves 4

beer and herb prawns

see variations page 77

I like to serve these juicy prawns with glasses of dark beer to complement the smoky flavours of the marinade.

900 g (2 lbs) peeled and deveined prawns
330 ml (12 fl oz) dark beer
2 cloves garlic, pressed
2 tbsp chopped fresh chives
2 tbsp chopped fresh parsley

1½ tsp sea salt
½ tsp freshly ground black pepper
Shredded lettuce
2 spring onions, thinly sliced

Combine all ingredients except the lettuce and spring onions in a bowl. Cover and chill for 3 to 4 hours, stirring occasionally. Drain.

Prepare a medium-hot barbecue. Place the shrimp in a heavy-based frying pan or wok and place over the grill. Cook the prawns until pink and tender, about 2 minutes on each side, or less for small prawns. Do not overcook or the prawns will become tough. Serve the prawns on shredded lettuce and sprinkle with sliced spring onions.

Serves 8

citrus-grilled scallops

see variations page 78

You should remove the corals from your scallops before preparing this dish, but don't discard them: sautéed with butter and garlic, they make a delicious snack.

235 ml (8 fl oz) water
235 ml (8 fl oz) chardonnay
4 tbsp fresh lemon juice
1 tbsp unsalted butter
1 tbsp clear honey
Pinch of sea salt

1 clove garlic, pressed
2 tsp cornflour, dissolved in 2 tbsp water
12 scallops, halved widthways
Melted butter, as needed
Chopped fresh parsley

In a small saucepan, combine the water, wine, lemon juice, butter, honey, salt and garlic. Place over medium heat, bring to the boil and boil until reduced by almost half, stirring frequently. Add enough of the cornflour solution to thicken the sauce. Remove from the heat and keep warm.

Grill the scallops over high heat for about 3 minutes on each side, brushing frequently with melted butter. Do not overcook, or they will toughen. Remove the scallops from the grill. Place 6 scallop halves on each plate. Pour the citrus sauce over the scallops and garnish with parsley.

Serves 4

grilled catfish

see variations page 79

Catfish are named for their 'whiskers'. The flavour is far finer than this unappetising name might suggest; catfish are valued by gourmets from the USA to Indonesia. You could substitute haddock if preferred.

Six 175 g (6 oz) catfish fillets
1 tbsp garlic salt

1 tsp white pepper
2 to 3 tbsp extra-virgin olive oil

Prepare the barbecue. Sprinkle the fish fillets with the garlic salt and pepper. Dip them in olive oil and grill over a high heat until the fish flakes easily (about 4 to 6 minutes per side). Be very careful when turning as catfish is very delicate; you might consider using a wire grill basket. Serve the fish with salsa, tartare sauce or herbed mustard.

Serves 6

variations

brown sugar-cured salmon

see base recipe page 47

lemon and basil salmon
Replace the brown sugar cure with 235 ml (8 fl oz) each of lemon yogurt and fresh basil leaves. Marinate for 2 hours and proceed to grill as in the base recipe.

mayonnaise and dill salmon
Replace the brown sugar cure with 235 ml (8 fl oz) mayonnaise and 1 tablespoon dried dill. Marinate for 2 hours and proceed to grill as in the base recipe.

maple barbecued salmon
Omit the brown sugar cure. Grill the salmon as in the base recipe and serve with a sauce made by blending together 225 g (8 oz) unsalted butter at room temperature and 235 ml (8 fl oz) maple syrup.

profanity salmon
Replace the brown sugar cure with 120 ml (4 fl oz) mayonnaise, 3 tablespoons teriyaki sauce, 1 teaspoon wasabi paste (you can substitute horseradish if desired) and salt and pepper to taste. Marinate for 2 hours and proceed to grill as in the base recipe.

juniper sugar-cured salmon
Prepare the base recipe, adding 2 teaspoons crushed juniper berries to the sugar cure.

grilled herby lemon salmon

see base recipe page 48

tequila and lime grilled salmon steaks
Replace the marinade with a mixture of 120 ml (4 fl oz) tequila; 60 ml (2 fl oz) each of fresh lime juice, triple sec, extra-virgin olive oil and chopped fresh coriander; and 4 large cloves garlic, chopped.

grilled teriyaki salmon steaks
Replace the marinade with a mixture of 120 ml (4 fl oz) each of soy sauce, sweet sherry or mirin and sugar; and 1 teaspoon each ground ginger and garlic granules.

grilled salmon steaks with marmalade dijon marinade
Replace the marinade with a marmalade dijon marinade made by heating gently in a saucepan 120 ml (4 fl oz) orange marmalade, 1 tablespoon Dijon mustard, ¹/₂ teaspoon garlic granules and ¹/₂ teaspoon ground ginger. Leave to cool, then marinate and grill salmon as in the base recipe.

salmon steaks with hoisin marinade
Replace the marinade with a hoisin marinade made by mixing 60 ml (2 fl oz) hoisin sauce, 2 tablespoons clear honey, 2 tablespoons fresh orange juice and ¹/₄ teaspoon mild chilli powder.

variations

'hot' grilled trout

see base recipe page 51

cajun-grilled trout with apple salsa
Omit the marinade. Instead dust the trout with Cajun spice mix before barbecuing, and serve the cooked fish with apple salsa. Garnish with fresh herbs and lemon wedges.

sesame-grilled trout
Replace the marinade with a mixture of 60 ml (2 fl oz) fresh lemon juice, 2 tablespoons unsalted butter, 3 tablespoons chopped fresh parsley, 2 tablespoons toasted sesame seeds, 1 tablespoon Tabasco sauce and sea salt to taste.

grilled spicy trout
Replace the marinade with an Asian-flavoured paste: mix 2 tablespoons fresh lemon juice; 1 tablespoon each of toasted ground cumin, chilli powder and vegetable oil; 1 teaspoon garam masala; and sea salt and freshly ground black pepper to taste. Pat this paste onto the fish before grilling.

grilled trout with thai sweet glaze
Replace the marinade with a Thai glaze: mix 6 tablespoons hoisin sauce, 3 tablespoons clear honey, 3 chopped shallots, 2 tablespoons rice vinegar, 1 tablespoon Thai fish sauce, 1 tablespoon dark soy sauce, 1 tablespoon grated fresh ginger, 2 pressed large cloves garlic and ¼ teaspoon Chinese five-spice powder. Brush both sides of the fish with this glaze before cooking.

grilled tilapia

see base recipe page 52

grilled tilapia with spinach and cherry tomatoes
Prepare the base recipe. Make a vegetable garnish for the grilled tilapia. Sauté 1 thinly sliced spring onion and 450 g (1 lb) fresh spinach. Cook until wilted, then stir in 225 g (8 oz) halved cherry tomatoes. Serve with the fish.

african tilapia
Omit the lime and mayonnaise coating. Make an African-flavored marinade by combining 235 ml (8 fl oz) olive oil; 1 small onion, chopped fine; 1 red pepper, chopped; juice and zest of 1 lemon; 1 tablespoon vinegar; 2 teaspoons cayenne pepper or crushed chillies; and 1 teaspoon sea salt. Marinate the tilapia for 2 hours, drain and grill as in the base recipe.

spicy grilled tilapia with aïoli
Omit the lime and mayonnaise coating. Before grilling, rub the tilapia with 1 teaspoon each of garlic granules, onion granules and toasted ground cumin, and 2 tablespoons chilli powder. Make an aïoli by whisking together 350 ml (12 fl oz) mayonnaise, 6 pressed garlic cloves, ½ tablespoon lemon juice, 1½ tablespoons Dijon mustard and ¾ teaspoon dried tarragon. Grill as in the base recipe.

lime and basil tilapia
Omit the lime and mayonnaise coating. Before grilling, marinate the tilapia for 2 hours in a mixture of 60 ml (2 fl oz) olive oil, the juice and zest of 2 limes, 1 tablespoon chopped fresh basil, 2 teaspoons bourbon, 1 teaspoon sea salt and freshly ground black pepper to taste.

variations

grilled swordfish steaks with citrus salsa

see base recipe page 54

grilled swordfish with fresh tomato and herb salsa
Replace the citrus salsa with a tomato salsa: mix 4 large plum tomatoes, peeled, seeded and diced; 4 tablespoons chopped fresh basil; 2 tablespoons chopped fresh marjoram; 1 chopped shallot; 1 teaspoon freshly ground black pepper; and salt to taste.

grilled swordfish with roast red pepper
Omit the citrus baste and salsa. Instead, marinate the swordfish for 2 hours in a mixture of 2 tablespoons fresh lemon juice and 235 ml (8 fl oz) olive oil. Grill as in the base recipe and, serve with 4 roasted red peppers, peeled, seeded and cut into strips; 1 tablespoon chopped fresh parsley; and salt and pepper to taste.

grilled ginger swordfish
Omit the citrus baste and salsa. Instead, marinate swordfish for 2 hours in a mixture of 120 ml (4 fl oz) olive oil, 3 tablespoons soy sauce, 3 tablespoons dry sherry and 1 tablespoon grated fresh ginger. Remove from marinade and barbecue as in the base recipe, brushing often with the marinade.

grilled dijon swordfish steaks
Omit the citrus baste and salsa. Marinate the swordfish for 2 hours in a mixture of 2 tablespoons Dijon mustard, 2 tablespoons olive oil, 1 tablespoon melted butter and 1 tablespoon white wine vinegar. Remove from the marinade and barbecue as in the base recipe, brushing often with the marinade. Serve with tartare sauce.

grilled halibut with pineapple

see base recipe page 55

grilled halibut with tomato, cucumber, and lemon sauce
Omit lime marinade and pineapple. Instead, whisk together 1 teaspoon grated lemon zest,
1½ tablespoons fresh lemon juice, ½ teaspoon dried oregano and 60 ml (2 fl oz) olive oil.
Stir into this mixture 175 g (6 oz) thinly sliced and seeded cherry tomatoes and 115 g (4 oz)
thinly sliced and seeded cucumber. Pour this sauce over the grilled halibut before serving.

grilled halibut with garlic butter
Omit lime marinade and pineapple. Instead, season the fish before cooking with a rub made
from ½ teaspoon each garlic granules, paprika, onion granules, lemon pepper and salt. Mix
together 3 tablespoons melted butter, 1½ tablespoons olive oil, 1 tablespoon chopped fresh
parsley and 2 pressed cloves garlic. Brush this garlic butter over the fish before grilling.

grilled chinese halibut
Omit lime marinade and pineapple. Instead, mix 1 tablespoon grated fresh ginger, 3 chopped
spring onions, 2 tablespoons light soy sauce, 2 tablespoons Chinese rice wine or dry sherry
and 1 tablespoon each soy sauce and Chinese sesame oil. Marinate the halibut in this
mixture for 2 hours before grilling. Garnish with 2 tablespoons chopped fresh coriander.

grilled blue cheese halibut
Omit lime marinade and pineapple. Instead, combine 115 g (4 oz) crumbled blue cheese,
475 ml (16 fl oz) buttermilk, 355 ml (12 fl oz) mayonnaise and water to thin if needed.
Reserve some of the marinade to use as a sauce. Garnish with 1 red onion, sliced and grilled.

variations

grilled shark to die for

see base recipe page 57

anticucho-style grilled shark

Replace the marinade with a blend of 120 ml (4 fl oz) soy sauce; 2 pickled jalapeños;
2 tablespoons each of chopped fresh coriander and parsley; 60 ml (2 fl oz) each of fresh
lime juice and vegetable oil; and 1 teaspoon cracked black pepper. Proceed with the base
recipe. Garnish the grilled steaks with lime wedges, sliced avocado and spicy tomato salsa.

marinated grilled shark

Replace the marinade with a mixture of 5 tablespoons fresh lime juice, 60 ml (2 fl oz)
teriyaki sauce, 2 tablespoons olive oil, 1 tablespoon light brown sugar, ½ teaspoon coarse
ground black pepper and ½ teaspoon paprika.

asian-grilled shark steak

Replace the marinade with a mixture of 2 tablespoons soy sauce, 3 tablespoons fresh
lemon juice, 2 tablespoons olive oil, 1 tablespoon sesame oil, 1 tablespoon mustard and
1 teaspoon sugar.

herbed shark steaks

Omit the marinade. Rub the shark all over with 6 pressed garlic cloves. Mix together
2 tablespoons lemon juice, 1 tablespoon fresh oregano, 1 tablespoon chopped fresh parsley,
1 teaspoon fresh dill and salt and pepper to taste. Marinate the garlic-rubbed shark for
2 hours and drain. Grill as in the base recipe.

mexican grilled red snapper

see base recipe page 58

grilled red snapper
Replace the marinade with a mixture of 4 tablespoons soy sauce, 2 teaspoons fresh lime juice,
1 tablespoon lemon pepper, 2 teaspoons garlic granules and 1 teaspoon sea salt.

grilled snapper with shallot butter
Replace whole snapper with 900 g (2 lbs) red snapper fillets, skin on. Replace marinade with a
mixture of 2 tablespoons olive oil, sea salt to taste, ½ teaspoon lemon zest, juice of ½ lemon,
2 tablespoons melted butter, 1 teaspoon dried tarragon, 1 tablespoon balsamic vinegar
1 chopped large shallot, cracked black pepper to taste and 1 pressed clove garlic. Grill as in the
base recipe.

grilled red snapper with soy sauce and avocado
Replace fish with 900 g (2 lbs) red snapper fillets. Marinate in a mixture of 4 tablespoons fresh
lemon juice, 1 tablespoon grated fresh ginger and 1 chopped large shallot. Grill as in base recipe.
Serve fish with a sauce made by blending together 1 tablespoon clover honey, 1 tablespoon soy
sauce, 4 tablespoons water and 1 tablespoon tahini. Garnish with 1 diced avocado.

grilled red snapper with crunchy red relish
Prepare the base recipe. Serve the grilled fish with a relish: sauté 2 chopped red peppers,
1 diced onion and 2 cloves chopped garlic in 115 g (4 oz) unsalted butter. Mix in 55 g (2 oz)
chopped toasted pecans; 200 g (7 oz) plum tomatoes, seeded and diced; 60 ml (2 fl oz) tomato
and chilli salsa; 4 tablespoons chopped fresh basil; and 1 tablespoon red wine vinegar.

grilled citrus tuna

see base recipe page 61

seared tuna in wasabi sauce
Omit the citrus marinade. Grill the tuna as in the base recipe. Serve with a sauce made by sautéeing together 285 ml (10 fl oz) white wine, 2 tablespoons white wine vinegar and 2 chopped shallots. Simmer until reduced to 60 ml (2 fl oz). Strain out the shallots. Add 1 tablespoon each of wasabi paste and soy sauce. Stir in 225 g (8 oz) melted butter and 8 tablespoons each of chopped fresh coriander and parsley. Serve with the grilled tuna.

grilled tuna in anchovy sauce
Omit the marinade. Grill the tuna as in the base recipe. Serve with an anchovy sauce made by heating gently together one 55 g (2 oz) can anchovies, drained; 10 black olives, stoned and chopped; 2 large cloves garlic, pressed; 60 ml (2 fl oz) white wine or chicken broth; 2 tablespoons chopped fresh parsley; 2 tablespoons fresh lemon juice; and 2 tablespoons capers, drained.

gourmet pepper-grilled tuna
Replace the citrus marinade with a pepper rub: brush the tuna with olive oil and then roll in a coating made from 1 tablespoon coarse ground tri-coloured peppercorns, 1 tablespoon sea salt, and 1 tablespoon grated lemon zest. Grill tuna as in the base recipe.

blackened tuna steaks
Replace the marinade with a mixture of 60 ml (2 fl oz) olive oil, 2 tablespoons fresh lime juice and 1 tablespoon Dijon mustard. Replace paprika rub with 2 tablespoons dried coriander, 1 tablespoon chilli powder and 1 teaspoon each of cracked black pepper and mustard seeds.

variations

beer and herb prawns

see base recipe page 62

herb-grilled prawns
Replace the marinade with a mixture of 60 ml (2 fl oz) each of Italian salad dressing and olive oil, 4 pressed cloves garlic, 1 tablespoon each of chopped fresh basil and dried thyme and chilli sauce to taste.

grilled prawns primavera
Cook the prawns as directed, without marinating first. Serve with linguine, the sauce recipe below and a mixture of grilled vegetables such as button mushrooms, peppers and onions. For the pasta sauce, heat two 400 g (14 oz) tins tomatoes, 2 tablespoons unsalted butter, juice of $1/2$ lemon, 1 tablespoon basil leaves and $1/4$ teaspoon each of black pepper, crushed chillies and dried marjoram. Omit the lettuce and sliced onions.

simple grilled prawns
Grill the prawns as directed, without marinating first. Drizzle over the cooked prawns a mixture of 115 g (4 oz) melted butter, 3 tablespoons fresh lemon juice, 2 tablespoons Worcestershire sauce, 1 tablespoon Tabasco sauce or to taste and $1/4$ teaspoon cayenne pepper.

grilled cajun peppered prawns
Replace marinade with a mixture of 225g (8 oz) melted butter; 1 clove garlic, pressed; $1/2$ teaspoon each of ground bay leaf, dried rosemary, basil, oregano, salt, cayenne pepper, nutmeg and paprika; 1 tablespoon freshly ground black pepper; and 2 tablespoons fresh lemon juice.

variations

citrus-grilled scallops

see base recipe page 65

grilled scallop kebabs
Omit the citrus marinade. Thread the raw scallop halves onto water-soaked bamboo skewers, alternating them with pieces of red pepper, green pepper and small whole onions. Before grilling, roll the kebabs in a mixture of 1 teaspoon *fines herbes* or Italian seasoning, 1 teaspoon lemon pepper, ½ teaspoon garlic granules, ¼ teaspoon sea salt and 2 tablespoons extra-virgin olive oil.

scallops grilled on rosemary
Replace citrus marinade with a rosemary marinade. Mix 2 tablespoons olive oil, 1 teaspoon chopped fresh rosemary, 2 pressed large cloves garlic, and sea salt and black pepper to taste. Grill the marinated scallops on a bed of fresh rosemary sprigs. Garnish with lemon wedges.

grilled scallops with ham and basil
Omit the citrus marinade. Make a marinade by sautéing 1 roughly chopped and seeded mild chilli, 1 pressed large clove garlic, 2 tablespoons olive oil and the juice of 3 limes. Thread the marinated scallops onto water-soaked skewers, alternating with basil leaves and strips of sliced ham.

caribbean scallops
Replace the citrus marinade with a rub made from 2 tablespoons onion granules; 1 teaspoon dry mustard; ½ teaspoon each of ground allspice, ground cinnamon, and crushed chillies; ¼ teaspoon garlic granules; 60 ml (2 fl oz) olive oil; and salt to taste.

grilled catfish

see base recipe page 66

creole-grilled catfish
Omit everything except the catfish. Grill the fish as in the base recipe. Make a sauce for the cooked fillets by blending together 8 tablespoons butter, melted; 1 large clove garlic, pressed; 60 ml (2 fl oz) olive oil; the juice of 1 lemon; 1 tablespoon Creole seasoning; and 1 teaspoon each of white pepper and lemon pepper.

grilled smoky catfish
Omit everything except the catfish. Marinate the catfish for 2 hours in 5 tablespoons soy sauce, 3 tablespoons vegetable oil, 1 clove garlic, pressed and 1 teaspoon grated fresh ginger. Grill the fish as in the base recipe.

grilled marinated catfish
Omit everything except the catfish. Marinate the catfish for 2 hours in 2 tablespoons olive oil, 1 tablespoon red wine vinegar, 1 tablespoon grated onion, $\frac{1}{2}$ teaspoon sea salt, $\frac{1}{4}$ teaspoon fine ground black pepper, and 4 tablespoons vegetable oil. Grill the fish as in the base recipe.

barbecued catfish
Omit everything except the catfish. Marinate the fish in 5 tablespoons extra-virgin olive oil, 2 teaspoons Worcestershire sauce, 1 teaspoon garlic granules, 1 teaspoon celery salt and a dash of Tabasco sauce. Grill the fish as in the base recipe and serve with bottled barbecue sauce.

chargrilled chicken and poultry

Crisp-skinned and tender-fleshed poultry is one of

barbecue's greatest pleasures.

whole barbecued chicken

see variations page 102

A plump whole chicken (free-range if possible) cooks to tender perfection on the grill.

1.6 to 2 kg (3$\frac{1}{2}$ to 4$\frac{1}{2}$ lb) whole chicken
for the marinade
235 ml (8 fl oz) Italian salad dressing
60 ml (2 fl oz) cider vinegar
1 tsp garlic granules
1 tsp sea salt
$\frac{1}{2}$ tsp crushed dried chillies
for the rub
2 tbsp granulated sugar
2 tbsp light brown sugar
2 tbsp seasoned salt

1 tbsp garlic salt
1 tbsp celery salt
2 tbsp paprika
2 tsp chilli powder
1 tbsp finely ground black pepper
1 tsp ground allspice
$\frac{1}{2}$ tsp dried basil
$\frac{1}{4}$ tsp dried tarragon
$\frac{1}{4}$ tsp mild chilli powder
for the glaze
475 ml (16 fl oz) barbecue sauce

Discard the giblets from the chicken. Rinse the chicken inside and out, and pat dry with kitchen paper. Combine the marinade ingredients and blend well. Place the chicken in a polythene bag and pour the marinade over it. Marinate for 4 hours in the refrigerator. Meanwhile, combine the rub ingredients and blend well. Set aside.

Remove the chicken from the marinade. Blot off the excess marinade with kitchen paper and season the chicken inside and out with the rub. Cook using the indirect method at 110°C to 120°C (230°F to 250°F) for 3 to 5 hours, depending on the size of the chicken. Glaze with barbecue sauce for the last 30 minutes of the cooking process.

Serves 6

herbed beer can chicken

see variations page 103

Steaming a chicken over a half-filled beer can infuses it with a delicious flavour.

for the rub
2 tbsp granulated sugar
2 tbsp garlic salt
1 tbsp paprika
1 tsp dried thyme
1 tsp ground black pepper
1 tsp grated lemon zest

$\frac{1}{4}$ tsp dried rosemary
1 whole chicken 1.8 to 2.3 kg (4 to 5 lbs)
One 350 ml (12 fl oz) can beer (room
    temperature)
1 clove garlic, chopped
1 sprig fresh rosemary, chopped
1 tsp dried thyme

Combine all the rub ingredients in a small mixing bowl and set aside. Remove the giblets from the chicken. Sprinkle all over with rub, including inside the cavity. Open the can of beer and discard half of it. Place the chopped garlic, rosemary and thyme in the can. Make sure to pierce two more holes into the top of beer can. Place the chicken over the can.

Preheat the grill. Place the bird on the grill rack, balanced on the beer can. Grill over indirect medium heat for 2$\frac{1}{2}$ to 3$\frac{1}{2}$ hours or until the internal temperature of the thigh is 75°C to 82°C (165°F to 180°F).

Wearing oven gloves, carefully remove the chicken and the can from the grill, being careful not to spill the beer – it will be hot. Let the chicken rest for about 10 minutes before lifting it from the can. Discard the beer can. Cut the chicken into serving pieces. Serve warm.

Serves 4

apple-raisin stuffed chicken thighs

see variations page 104

Stuffing chicken thighs is not difficult to do, and helps keep the meat tender and full of fruity flavour.

2 tbsp raisins or prunes
1 tbsp dark rum
1 firm cooking apple
olive oil
1 onion, chopped
2 tsp granulated sugar

$1/2$ tsp ground cinnamon
$1/4$ tsp ground allspice
55 g (2 oz) fresh wholemeal breadcrumbs
8 boneless chicken thighs
60 ml (2 fl oz) apple juice

Put the raisins or prunes in a small bowl and sprinkle with rum. Let the fruit stand for 20 minutes. Peel, core and chop the apple. Heat a nonstick frying pan, brushed with a little olive oil. Sauté the onion and apple, covered, for about 5 minutes over medium heat, stirring frequently. Mix the sugar, cinnamon and allspice together, and sprinkle over the apple mixture. Toss in the breadcrumbs and raisins or prunes. Divide the stuffing and fill pockets in the chicken thighs, securing with cocktail sticks.

Prepare a medium-hot grill. Add some chunks of applewood if using a charcoal grill. Brush the grill racks with oil. Brush the chicken with apple juice. Place the chicken on the grill rack, skin-side down; cook for 6 to 8 minutes until the chicken browns. Turn over, brush on more apple juice and cook for about 6 more minutes or until cooked through. The grilling time depends on the size and thickness of the thighs.

Serves 4

grilled cornish game hens

see variations page 105

Tender Cornish game hens are small enough that everyone can enjoy their own bird.

3 tbsp olive oil
2 tsp chilli powder
2 tbsp chopped fresh thyme
2 tbsp onion granules
1 tsp garlic granules

1 tbsp sea salt
$\frac{1}{2}$ tsp freshly ground black pepper
Four 680 to 900 g (1$\frac{1}{2}$ to 2 lb) Cornish
    game hens (or poussins), each cut in half
    lengthways

Mix the oil and seasonings in a small bowl to form a paste. Brush the paste over the hens. Marinate for 30 minutes at room temperature.

Grill the hens on a barbecue preheated to medium until cooked through and the juices run clear when the thickest part of the thigh is pierced with a fork. Transfer to a platter and serve.

Serves 4

grilled herbed duck breasts

see variations page 106

The natural oil in duck breasts means they withstand perfectly the searing heat of a grill.

120 ml (4 fl oz) olive oil
Juice of 1 lemon
4 juniper berries, crushed
1 tbsp Worcestershire sauce
2 cloves garlic, pressed
1 tsp dried thyme

1 tsp ground bay leaves
$\frac{1}{2}$ tsp onion granules
$\frac{1}{2}$ tsp freshly ground black pepper
$\frac{1}{4}$ tsp paprika
4 duck breasts

Put all ingredients except the duck breasts in a small saucepan. Simmer for 5 to 7 minutes. Remove the mixture from the heat and allow to cool. Place the duck breasts in a resealable polythene bag. Pour $\frac{1}{2}$ the cooled herb mixture over the duck, seal the bag, and allow to marinate in the refrigerator for 6 to 8 hours. Reserve the remaining marinade.

Preheat the grill to medium-high. Remove the duck breasts from their polythene bag, discarding the marinade. Place the duck on a lightly oiled grill rack. Grill for 3 minutes, baste with the reserved quarter of the marinade mixture, and turn. Continue to cook, basting every 3 minutes, until the internal temperature of the breasts reaches 63˚C (145˚F). Remove from the heat, slice and serve.

Serves 6

hot and sticky summertime chicken

see variations page 107

Here's an easy recipe for spatchcocked – split and grilled – chicken.

1.6 to 1.8 kg (3½ to 4½ lb) whole chicken
for the marinade
330 ml (11 fl oz) can Dr Pepper
10 cloves garlic, pressed
3 whole chillies
2 tbsp sweet chilli sauce
1 onion, grated
2 tbsp chopped fresh coriander

2 tbsp chopped fresh parsley
2 tsp sea salt
for the glaze
120 ml (4 fl oz) clear honey
2 tbsp Dijon mustard
2 tbsp grated fresh ginger
1 tbsp grated orange zest
1 tbsp grated lime zest

Remove the giblets from inside the chicken. Rinse and dry the chicken. Spatchcock it by cutting down the length of the spine with a sharp knife and removing the backbone. In the centre of the breast on the inside is a white piece of gristle, on the keel bone. Cut into the centre of it, place your thumbs on either side of the breast, and pop out the keel bone. Flatten the bird. Place in a large resealable polythene bag. Combine the marinade ingredients in a bowl. Pour over the chicken and seal the bag. Refrigerate for a minimum of 3 hours, though overnight is better.

In a small bowl, combine the glaze ingredients. Preheat the barbecue to medium heat. Place the bird on the grill rack, bone-side down. Discard the bag and the marinade. Cook the chicken for about 15 to 20 minutes on each side. When its internal temperature reaches 75°C (165°F), start to brush on the glaze. Continue brushing on the glaze until it is used up and the meat reaches 77°C (170°F.) Remove the chicken from the grill and leave to rest in a warm place, covered, for 10 minutes before cutting.

Serves 4

grilled turkey steaks with rosemary marinade

see variations page 108

Turkey brushed with a mellow herbed marinade is a perfect barbecue dish for autumn.

2 spring onions, sliced thinly
120 ml (4 fl oz) fresh orange juice
3 tbsp olive oil
2 tbsp chopped fresh rosemary leaves
2 tbsp balsamic vinegar

1 tsp grated lemon zest
2 tsp lemon juice
1 tbsp clear honey
$\frac{1}{2}$ tsp sea salt
4 turkey breast steaks

Mix all ingredients except the turkey in a resealable polythene bag. Remove 60 ml (2 fl oz) and set aside. Add the turkey steaks to the marinade in the bag, seal and shake to mix.

Marinate the turkey for at least one hour. Remove the turkey from the marinade and place on a grill rack over a medium heat. Grill for 5 minutes and turn to grill the other side for an additional 3 to 5 minutes. Brush the turkey with the reserved marinade during grilling. Remove from the grill and serve.

Serves 4

honey-citrus chicken

see variations page 109

Avoid the potential blandness of chicken breasts by marinating them in this simple sweet and sour mixture for an hour or so before cooking.

4 chicken breasts
Juice of 1 orange
Juice of 1 lime
Juice of 1 lemon

3 tbsp clear honey
2 tbsp olive oil
$^1/_2$ tsp Tabasco sauce

Gently pound the chicken breasts between sheets of clingfilm, with your hand or a meat mallet, just enough to make the breasts even in thickness. Marinate the meat in the citrus juices, honey, oil and Tabasco for about an hour at room temperature.

Grill the chicken on a grill preheated to medium for about 5 to 7 minutes per side, turning once, or until cooked through. When pierced with a fork, the juices should run clear.

Serves 4

barbecued quail

see variations page 110

Plump little quails are always succulent. Serve them with wedges of lemon to add a sharp note to the predominantly sweet marinade.

85 g (3 oz) finely sliced spring onions
60 ml (2 fl oz) clear honey
2 tbsp Worcestershire sauce
4 large cloves garlic, pressed
1 tbsp dry mustard

2 tsp chilli powder
235 ml (8 fl oz) dry white wine
Sea salt and freshly ground black pepper to taste
Four 115 to 140 g (4 to 5 oz) semi-boneless quail

Combine all the ingredients except the quail in a saucepan. Heat for about 15 minutes over a medium heat. Remove from the heat and cool to room temperature.

Place the quail in a baking dish and pour about two-thirds of the marinade over them. Reserve the rest of the marinade for basting while grilling. Preheat a grill to medium.

Marinate the quail for about 30 minutes at room temperature and then grill for about 3 to 4 minutes on each side, basting regularly with the reserved third of the marinade. Remove when the flesh is firm and the juices run clear from the leg when pierced. Serve at once.

Serves 2

peach-ginger turkey cutlets

see variations page 111

Turkey cutlets are low in fat, so they are an excellent choice for those who want to eat healthily.

1 tbsp finely grated root ginger
3 tbsp soy sauce
5 tbsp rice vinegar

5 tbsp olive oil
115 g (4 oz) peach jam
Four 170 g (6 oz) turkey cutlets

Mix all the ingredients except the turkey together for a marinade. Reserve 60 ml (2 fl oz) for basting. Place the cutlets and the rest of the marinade in a large resealable polythene bag or baking dish. Refrigerate for 30 minutes, turning occasionally.

Heat and lightly oil the grill. Drain the cutlets. Grill for 5 minutes on each side, basting occasionally with the reserved marinade, until cooked thoroughly and the cutlets have reached an internal temperature of 77°C (170°F).

Serves 4

hot jamaican jerk chicken

see variations page 112

The jerk spice paste is exceptionally fiery, so you may want to use fewer chillies.

3 large Scotch bonnet chillies
3 spring onions, chopped
2 tbsp white wine vinegar
2 tbsp dried rosemary
2 tbsp dried basil
2 tbsp dried thyme

2 tbsp mustard seeds
2 tbsp dried parsley
1 tsp fresh lime juice
1 tsp yellow mustard
Sea salt and black pepper to taste
12 chicken drumsticks

Purée all the ingredients, except the chicken, to make a paste. Refrigerate for 2 hours. Submerge the chicken legs in the mixture and be sure they are well coated. Then grill the chicken legs over a very low heat for 40 to 50 minutes.

Or, to cook direct, cook the drumsticks on a grill preheated to medium, for 10 minutes per side or until the skin is crispy and golden brown. The drumsticks are done when the juices run clear when pierced in the thickest part. Remove from the grill and tent with foil. Leave to rest for 5 minutes before serving.

Serves 4

turkey drumsticks with fruity salsa

see base recipe page 113

This Mexican-style salsa adds a zesty and intriguing note to the simply grilled turkey.

6 small turkey drumsticks
for the marinade
120 ml (4 fl oz) fresh lime juice
60 ml (2 fl oz) fresh chopped sage
3 tbsp white wine vinegar
2 tbsp granulated sugar
120 ml (4 fl oz) olive oil
for the salsa
1 small pineapple, peeled and diced

1 small papaya, peeled and diced
1 medium lime, peeled and diced
1 small red pepper, seeded and diced
1 medium red onion, chopped
2 finely chopped fresh red chillies
4 tbsp chopped fresh coriander
3 tbsp fresh lime juice
Sea salt to taste

Combine the lime juice, sage, vinegar, sugar and oil in a small mixing bowl. Place the turkey drumsticks in a large resealable polythene bag, pour the marinade over the turkey and marinate overnight in the refrigerator. Remove the turkey from the marinade. Cook the turkey pieces on a preheated and lightly oiled grill rack, turning every 10 to 15 minutes. They are cooked when the juices run clear or when the internal temperature reaches 77°C (170°F).

Meanwhile, combine the pineapple, papaya, lime, pepper and onion in a bowl. Stir in the chillies, coriander, lime juice and salt. Serve the salsa as an accompaniment to the turkey.

Serves 6

variations

whole barbecued chicken

see base recipe page 81

moroccan-style smoked chicken
Replace the rub with a glaze made from 4 tablespoons melted unsalted butter, 4 tablespoons clear honey, 2 teaspoons ground ginger, 1 teaspoon ground cinnamon, 1 teaspoon ground coriander, ¼ teaspoon ground turmeric, ⅛ teaspoon ground mace and sea salt and freshly ground black pepper to taste.

marinated barbecued chicken
Replace the rub with a marinade made by mixing 235 ml (8 fl oz) soy sauce, 120 ml (4 fl oz) cider vinegar, 2 pressed cloves garlic and 1 teaspoon each dried oregano and dried tarragon.

billy's barbecued chicken
Replace the rub with the following rub mixture: 1 tablespoon dark brown sugar; 1 tablespoon paprika; 1 teaspoon each of onion salt, garlic salt, celery salt and dry mustard; and ¼ teaspoon cayenne pepper.

spicy barbecued chicken
Replace the rub with the following rub mixture: 225 g (8 oz) light brown sugar; 1 tablespoon ground allspice; and 1 teaspoon each of ground thyme, dry mustard, garlic granules, ground ginger and cayenne pepper.

herbed beer can chicken

see base recipe page 82

dr pepper chicken barbecue
Substitute the following rub mixture: 1 tablespoon paprika, 1 teaspoon dry mustard, 1 teaspoon each of onion granules and sea salt, and ½ teaspoon each of garlic granules, ground coriander, ground cumin and freshly ground black pepper. Replace the beer can with a 330 ml (11 fl oz) can of Dr Pepper.

stout beer can chicken barbecue
Substitute the following rub mixture: 55g (2 oz) dark brown sugar; 4 tablespoons sweet paprika; 2 tablespoons ground black pepper; sea salt to taste; 1 tablespoon hickory smoked salt (optional); 2 teaspoons each of garlic granules, onion granules and celery seeds; and 1 teaspoon mild chilli powder. Replace the beer can with a 330 ml (11 fl oz) can of stout.

sweet california beer can chicken barbecue
Substitute the following rub mixture: 2 tablespoons light brown sugar, 1 tablespoon each of sugar and smoked paprika, 1½ teaspoons garlic granules, sea salt to taste, 1 teaspoon pepper, ½ teaspoon dry mustard and ¼ teaspoon each of cayenne pepper, dried ground sage and chicken seasoning. Replace the beer with a beer can half-filled with white wine.

cola can chicken barbecue
Substitute the following rub mixture: 1 teaspoon each of dry mustard, sea salt, garlic granules, pepper and onion granules, and 1 tablespoon paprika. Replace the beer can with a 330 ml (11 fl oz) can cola.

variations

apple-raisin stuffed chicken thighs

see base recipe page 85

grilled cajun chicken
Omit the apple-raisin stuffing. Instead, marinate the chicken thighs in 60 ml (2 fl oz) vegetable oil, 2 tablespoons Cajun spice mix, and sea salt and freshly ground black pepper to taste. Omit the apple juice, and glaze with 475 ml (16 fl oz) barbecue sauce.

oriental grilled chicken thighs
Omit the apple-raisin stuffing. Instead, marinate the thighs in 235 ml (8 fl oz) soy sauce, 120 ml (4 fl oz) dark brown sugar, 2 tablespoons peeled and chopped fresh ginger, 4 pressed large garlic cloves and 1 teaspoon Chinese five-spice powder.

chipotle-lime grilled chicken thighs
Omit the apple-raisin stuffing. Instead, marinate the thighs in 120 ml (4 fl oz) fresh lime juice; 120 ml (4 fl oz) olive oil; 2 tablespoons pickled chilli peppers, finely chopped; 1 tablespoon clear honey; and salt and freshly ground black pepper to taste.

hot and sticky grilled thighs with apricot glaze
Omit the apple-raisin stuffing and the apple juice. Instead, glaze the thighs as they cook with an apricot glaze. Warm gently together 235 ml (8 fl oz) apricot conserve, 120 ml (4 fl oz) white wine vinegar, 2 tablespoons light rum, 2 tablespoons hot mustard and 2 pressed large garlic cloves.

grilled cornish game hens

see base recipe page 86

citrus marinated cornish hens
Replace the spice paste with a marinade made by mixing 2 tablespoons olive oil, 120 ml (4 fl oz) fresh orange juice, 60 ml (2 fl oz) fresh lemon juice, 60 ml (2 fl oz) water, ½ onion, finely chopped, 1 teaspoon crumbled dried rosemary, ½ teaspoon dried thyme and 1 pressed clove garlic. Let the hens marinate for 2 hours.

john's grilled cornish game hens
Replace the spice paste with a rub made from 1 tablespoon garlic salt, 1 tablespoon lemon pepper and 1 teaspoon chicken seasoning.

grilled cornish hens with tarragon and dijon mustard
Replace the spice paste with a marinade made from 120 ml (4 fl oz) buttermilk, 3 tablespoons Dijon mustard, 2 tablespoons white wine vinegar, 2 chopped shallots, 1 tablespoon gin and 2 teaspoons dried tarragon. Let the hens marinate for 2 hours. Remove from the marinade and grill. Sprinkle the grilled hens with salt and pepper to taste.

grilled cornish hens with smoked paprika
Replace the spice paste with a rub made from 55 g (2 oz) light brown sugar; 1 tablespoon smoked paprika; 2 teaspoons chilli powder; 2 teaspoons ground cumin; 1 teaspoon each of dried oregano, sea salt, onion granules and cayenne pepper; ½ teaspoon garlic granules; and ½ teaspoon lemon pepper.

variations

grilled herbed duck breasts

see base recipe page 89

asian grilled duck breasts
Replace the marinade with one made by mixing 120 ml (4 fl oz) soy sauce, 60 ml (2 fl oz) red wine or cider, 2 tablespoons olive oil, 2 tablespoons light brown sugar, 1 tablespoon each of lemon juice and lime juice, ¼ teaspoon garlic granules, ⅛ teaspoon ground black pepper, and sea salt.

grilled duck breast with ginger, balsamic vinegar and orange sauce
Omit the marinade. Grill the unmarinated duck breasts, then serve with a sauce made by mixing 120 ml (4 fl oz) fresh orange juice, 355 ml (12 fl oz) chicken stock, 60 ml (2 fl oz) balsamic vinegar, 2 teaspoons grated fresh ginger, 4 tablespoons melted butter, ½ teaspoon sea salt, 1 teaspoon cracked black pepper and 1 teaspoon grated orange zest.

grilled duck breasts with plum glaze
Omit the herb marinade. Make a glaze by heating gently in a saucepan 4 tablespoons butter, 1 tablespoon garlic salt, 2 teaspoons coarse ground black pepper, 235 ml (8 fl oz) red plum jam, 235 ml (8 fl oz) hoisin sauce, 1 tablespoon grated fresh ginger, 1 teaspoon sea salt and ½ teaspoon finely ground black pepper. Brush the glaze onto the breasts as they cook.

chargrilled duck breasts with redcurrant glaze
Omit the herb marinade. Before grilling, top each duck breast with 1 slice apple-smoked bacon. Make a glaze by heating gently in a saucepan 2 beef bouillon cubes, 235 ml (8 fl oz) water, 2 tablespoons redcurrant jelly, ½ teaspoon dry mustard, 1 tablespoon sherry or brandy, ⅛ teaspoon dried marjoram, ¼ teaspoon dried oregano and the grated zest of an orange.

variations

hot and sticky summertime chicken

see base recipe page 90

oriental marinated smoked chicken
Replace the marinade with one made by combining 120 ml (4 fl oz) rice wine, 60 ml
(2 fl oz) sesame oil, 60 ml (2 fl oz) soy sauce, 2 tablespoons honey mustard, 5 tablespoons
light brown sugar, 2 dashes liquid smoke flavouring, 1 tablespoon grated orange zest,
2 teaspoons ground ginger, 2 teaspoons paprika, 1 teaspoon *fines herbes* and ¼ teaspoon
dried rosemary.

mary's barbecued chicken
Replace the marinade with a rub made by mixing together 1 tablespoon sugar, 1 tablespoon
caster sugar, 2 tablespoons sea salt, 1 teaspoon each of dry mustard and onion granules, and
½ teaspoon each of paprika, dried coriander, dried basil, garlic granules, ground coriander,
ground cumin and freshly ground black pepper.

peruvian grilled chicken
Replace the summertime marinade with one made by combining 5 tablespoons soy sauce,
2 tablespoons vegetable oil, 2 tablespoons fresh lime juice, 5 large pressed cloves garlic,
2 teaspoons toasted ground cumin, 1 tablespoon paprika and 1 teaspoon dried oregano.

easy grilled cajun chicken
Replace the summertime marinade with a rub made by mixing together 2 tablespoons
smoked paprika, 1 tablespoon garlic granules, 2 teaspoons sea salt, and 1 teaspoon each of
cayenne pepper, white pepper, black pepper, oregano, thyme and onion granules.

variations

grilled turkey steaks with rosemary marinade

see base recipe page 91

turkey steaks with sherry and lemon marinade
Substitute for the rosemary marinade a blend of 4 tablespoons each of soy sauce, olive oil and sherry; 2 tablespoons each of fresh lemon juice and grated onion; $\frac{1}{2}$ teaspoon ground ginger; pepper to taste; and a dash of seasoned salt.

tarragon turkey steaks
Substitute for the rosemary marinade a blend of 5 tablespoons olive oil, 2 tablespoons red wine vinegar, 1 tablespoon Dijon mustard, 1 large pressed clove garlic, 2 teaspoons crushed dried tarragon, $\frac{1}{2}$ teaspoon salt and $\frac{1}{4}$ teaspoon ground pepper.

redcurrant-glazed szechwan turkey steaks
Substitute for the rosemary marinade a glaze made by heating gently together 235 ml (8 fl oz) redcurrant jelly, 4 tablespoons hoisin sauce, 2 tablespoons light brown sugar, 2 tablespoons triple sec, 1 tablespoon grated fresh ginger, $\frac{1}{2}$ teaspoon chilli powder, 1 teaspoon sea salt, 1 teaspoon ground Szechwan peppercorns, $\frac{1}{2}$ teaspoon garlic granules and 2 tablespoons vegetable oil.

hoisin-glazed turkey steaks
Substitute for the rosemary marinade a glaze made by heating gently together 4 tablespoons hoisin sauce, 4 tablespoons fresh orange juice, 1 teaspoon garlic granules, 1 teaspoon onion granules, and $\frac{1}{2}$ teaspoon each of sea salt, freshly ground black pepper and cayenne pepper.

variations

honey-citrus chicken

see base recipe page 92

afghan chicken
Replace the marinade with an Afghan version, made by mixing 2 large pressed cloves garlic,
½ teaspoon sea salt, 475 ml (16 fl oz) plain whole-milk yogurt, 4 tablespoons lemon juice,
the pulp of 1 large lemon and ½ teaspoon cracked black pepper. Serve the chicken with
pitta bread.

apple-honey glazed chicken
Replace the marinade with a glaze made by mixing 5 tablespoons apple jelly, 1 tablespoon
clear honey, 1 tablespoon Dijon mustard, ½ teaspoon ground cinnamon and sea salt to taste.

athenian chicken on the grill
Replace the marinade with a Greek version, made by mixing 120 ml (4 fl oz) dry red wine;
120 ml (4 fl oz) olive oil; 4 tablespoons fresh lemon juice; 2 tablespoons dried oregano;
1 teaspoon each of dried thyme, dried basil leaves, grated lemon zest, sea salt; and
½ teaspoon ground black pepper.

grilled italian chicken breasts
Replace the marinade with an Italian version, made by mixing 2 pressed cloves garlic,
1 teaspoon toasted and crushed fennel seeds, 2 tablespoons fresh lemon juice, 2 tablespoons
olive oil, and sea salt and freshly ground black pepper to taste.

variations

barbecued quail

see base recipe page 95

grilled quail with jalapeño plum sauce
Replace the marinade with a glaze: 2½ tablespoons vegetable oil; 1 red onion, finely chopped, 1½ tablespoons pressed garlic; ½ fresh red chilli pepper, finely chopped, 680 g (1½ lbs) purple plums, stoned and diced; 2 teaspoons mild curry powder; ½ teaspoon ground allspice; 120 ml (4 fl oz) clear honey; 60 ml (2 fl oz) soy sauce; and the juice of 1 orange and 2 lemons. Heat all the glaze ingredients gently in a pan.

grilled quail with a garlic and juniper glaze
Replace the marinade with glaze. Mix 1 tablespoon each chopped garlic and crushed juniper berries; juice of 1 lemon, 4 tablespoons dry vermouth, ½ teaspoon dried thyme, 2 teaspoons rubbed sage, and sea salt and black pepper to taste. Marinate for 30 minutes. Glaze grilled quail with 4 tablespoons melted unsalted butter and 235 ml (8 fl oz) barbecue sauce, stirred together.

zesty garlic-lime quail
Replace the marinade with a spice paste made by combining 4 large pressed cloves garlic, 2 tablespoons light olive oil, 1 tablespoon grated lime zest, 2 teaspoons chopped fresh thyme leaves, and salt and pepper to taste. Rub into the quail and marinate for 30 minutes.

asian grilled quail
Replace the marinade with a Chinese marinade. Mix 4 tablespoons hoisin sauce; 3 tablespoons each of chilli-garlic sauce, dark sesame oil and clear honey; 2 tablespoons sesame seeds, 1 teaspoon ground ginger and ½ teaspoon Chinese five-spice powder. Marinate for 30 minutes.

peach–ginger turkey cutlets

see base recipe page 96

grilled mustard turkey cutlets
Replace the marinade with a sauce made by combining in a small bowl 2 tablespoons Dijon mustard, 2 teaspoons mayonnaise, 1 teaspoon fresh lemon juice, and pepper to taste. Garnish with a sprinkling of paprika and 2 tablespoons chopped fresh parsley.

grilled turkey cutlets with dijon sauce
Replace the marinade with a mustard version made by combining 60 ml (2 fl oz) vegetable oil, 60 ml (2 fl oz) clear honey, 2 tablespoons Dijon mustard, 1 teaspoon lemon zest, 2 tablespoons lemon juice, 1 pressed clove garlic, ¼ teaspoon dried thyme, and sea salt and freshly ground black pepper to taste. Reserve 60 ml (2 fl oz) marinade to use as a sauce.

teriyaki turkey cutlets
Replace the marinade with an Asian version made by combining 120 ml (4 fl oz) soy sauce, 60 ml (2 fl oz) sweet rice wine, 2 tablespoons clear honey, 2 teaspoons grated fresh ginger, 1 teaspoon grated orange zest, 1 teaspoon sesame oil and 2 cloves pressed garlic. Garnish with toasted sesame seeds.

spicy grilled turkey cutlets with pineapple rings
Replace the marinade with a Caribbean version made by combining a 525 g (20 oz) can pineapple rings, drained, 3 tablespoons honey, 1 tablespoon vegetable oil, ¼ teaspoon ground cinnamon, 2 tablespoons each of Jamaican jerk seasoning and soy sauce, 1 tablespoon each of lemon juice and dried onion, and ¼ teaspoon salt. Use to baste turkey.

variations

hot jamaican jerk chicken

see base recipe page 99

maple-barbecued chicken drumsticks
Instead of making the spice paste, glaze the chicken with the following mixture, which you have warmed gently in a saucepan: 120 ml (4 fl oz) chilli sauce, 120 ml (4 fl oz) maple syrup, 3 tablespoons cider vinegar, 3 tablespoons vegetable oil, 1 tablespoon prepared mustard, ½ teaspoon sea salt and ¼ teaspoon Tabasco sauce.

grilled chicken drumsticks
Instead of making the spice paste, marinate the chicken for 2 hours in the following mixture: 4 tablespoons each soy sauce, fresh lemon juice and sesame oil; 120 ml (4 fl oz) clear honey, 4 pressed cloves garlic, 2 tablespoons grated fresh ginger, 3 tablespoons vegetable oil, 1 teaspoon crushed dried chillies and pepper to taste.

simple grilled drumsticks
Instead of making the spice paste, rub the chicken with the following mixture before grilling: 4 teaspoons sea salt, 2 teaspoons smoked paprika, 1 teaspoon onion granules and ½ teaspoon each of dried thyme, garlic granules, dried basil and freshly ground pepper.

butch's lip-smacking chicken drumsticks
Instead of making the spice paste, marinate the chicken for 1 hour in the following mixture: 2 tablespoons ketchup; 2 tablespoons soy sauce; 1 tablespoon each of balsamic vinegar, clear honey, light brown sugar and Dijon mustard; the juice and zest of 1 orange; and sea salt and freshly ground black pepper to taste.

turkey drumsticks with fruity salsa

see base recipe page 100

mexican turkey drumsticks
Replace the salsa with a rub made from 2 teaspoons each of sea salt, finely ground black pepper and chilli powder, and ½ teaspoon each of ground cumin and garlic granules.

drumsticks in sweet and spicy barbecue sauce
Omit the salsa. Gently heat together 2 tablespoons light brown sugar, 235 ml (8 fl oz) ketchup, 4 tablespoons fresh lemon juice, 1 tablespoon each of onion granules and Worcestershire sauce, 1 tablespoon Dijon mustard, and 1 teaspoon each of chilli powder and cayenne pepper.

ginger-garlic barbecued turkey drumsticks
Omit the salsa. Heat together 120 ml (4 fl oz) light soy sauce, 2 tablespoons each of sherry and light brown sugar, 1 tablespoon grated root ginger, 2 teaspoons oil and 1 clove pressed garlic.

grilled turkey drumsticks
Omit the salsa. Heat 4 tablespoons fresh lemon juice; 2 tablespoons dark brown sugar; 1 tablespoon each of Worcestershire sauce, soy sauce and Dijon mustard; 1 teaspoon each of chilli powder and onion granules; and 235 ml (8 fl oz) tomato ketchup.

grilled herbed yogurt turkey drumsticks
Omit marinade and salsa. Instead, marinate drumsticks for 2 hours in mix of 235 ml (8 fl oz) Greek yogurt; 3 tablespoons each of Dijon mustard and clear honey; 2 teaspoons each of dried basil and sea salt; and ½ teaspoon each of dried thyme, dried oregano, dried dill and black pepper.

perfect pork and lamb

Succulent meaty grills are often regarded as the

centerpiece of a good barbecue – and here are

dozens of superb choices. The recipes in this chapter

will help you make the most of the sweet taste of

pork and the smoky flavour of lamb.

teriyaki pork burgers

see variations page 139

In Japanese, *teri* means sunshine and *yaki* means roast or grilled, so what could be more suitable for barbecuing?

680 g (1½ lbs) minced pork
4 tablespoons fine dry breadcrumbs
¼ tsp freshly ground black pepper
2 tbsp finely chopped onion
2 spring onions, thinly sliced

1 large clove garlic, pressed
2 tbsp soy sauce
2 tbsp orange juice
2 tsp ground ginger
1 tbsp light brown sugar

Prepare the barbecue to medium heat. Combine all the ingredients. Form into 4 to 6 patties. Grill over medium heat for 5 to 10 minutes per side or until no pink remains. Always cook minced pork to well done or 75°C (165°F). Serve on hamburger buns with your favourite condiments and garnishes, such as pickled gherkins, sliced onions, shredded lettuce and sliced tomatoes.

For a new taste sensation, serve on a hamburger bun with a layer of oranges, sliced kiwi fruit and sliced strawberries on top.

Makes 4–6 burgers

jerk barbecued ribs

see variations page 140

Caribbean jerk seasoning adds a zesty kick to pork ribs.

8 tbsp Jamaican jerk seasoning
1 tbsp light brown sugar
2 tbsp red wine vinegar
1.8 kg (4 lbs) pork spareribs
475 ml (16 fl oz) barbecue sauce

Combine the jerk seasoning, sugar and vinegar in a bowl. Remove ¼ of the mixture
and reserve. Add the ribs to the remaining marinade in the bowl and turn to coat them
thoroughly. Marinate for 3 to 4 hours or overnight in the refrigerator. Remove the ribs from
the marinade.

Preheat a barbecue to medium. Cook ribs for 2 to 2½ hours, turning and brushing frequently
with the reserved ¼ of the marinade. Brush and glaze the ribs with the barbecue sauce
during the last 15 minutes of cooking.

Serves 6

german-style barbecued pork sandwich

see variations page 141

Slathered with mustard and served with crunchy pickles, this sandwich is a delightful combination of tastes and textures.

Two 340 g (12 oz) pork tenderloins
3 tbsp German mustard, plus more for bread
Sea salt and freshly ground black pepper
1 long baguette (allow 15 cm [6 in] for
    each person)

4 to 8 tablespoons tomato ketchup
1 tbsp curry powder
Pickled cornichons or gherkins, sliced

Prepare grill to medium-high heat. Pat the tenderloins dry and rub with mustard. Sprinkle with salt and pepper and place on the grill. Grill for 10 minutes on each side, or until a thermometer inserted in the thickest part reads 68°C (155°F). Remove the tenderloins from the barbecue and leave to stand, loosely covered with foil, for about 10 minutes (the internal temperature will rise by 5 to 10 degrees).

Slice the baguette into four 15 cm (6 in) segments; slice open and spread with a little mustard. Slice the cooked pork very thinly and divide among the prepared baguette. Garnish with a mixture of the ketchup, curry powder and sliced cornichons or gherkins and serve.

Serves 4

black pepper pork steaks with treacle butter

see variations page 142

These peppered chops are an American favourite. Serve topped with the sweet butter.

55 g (2 oz) unsalted butter, softened
1 tbsp black treacle
1 tsp fresh lemon juice

4 tbsp coarsely ground black pepper
4 boneless pork loin steaks, 4 cm (1½ in) thick

In a small bowl, blend the butter, treacle and lemon juice with a fork. Cover the bowl and refrigerate until needed.

Trim the fat from the pork and rub them evenly on both sides with pepper. Grill the pork over a medium-hot grill for 12 to 15 minutes, turning once. To serve, top each pork steak with a tablespoon of the treacle butter.

Serves 4

st. louis pork steaks

see variations page 143

The seasoned cider vinegar leaves the pork steaks juicy and unbelievably tasty, which perhaps explains why in St. Louis they pull out the grill to make this classic dish even in midwinter!

Five 1.5 cm ($^1/_2$ in) pork shoulder steaks
2 tbsp seasoned salt, or to taste
1 tbsp seasoned pepper mix, or to taste

475 ml (16 fl oz) cider vinegar
375 ml (12 fl oz) water
475 ml (16 fl oz) barbecue sauce

Season the pork steaks on both sides with seasoned salt and seasoned pepper mix. In a large bowl, stir together the vinegar and water and season with seasoned salt and seasoned pepper mix to taste.

Preheat the barbecue to medium-low. Lightly oil the grill rack. Place the pork steaks on the grill. Baste the steaks with the vinegar mixture on both sides during the first 15 minutes of grilling. Continue to cook the steaks to desired doneness, allowing roughly 10 to 15 minutes more. Discard any remaining vinegar mixture at the end of cooking. Brush liberally with barbecue sauce on both sides to glaze the steaks, and cook for a minute or two before serving.

Serves 5

barbecued pork shoulder

see variations page 144

The triple flavouring in this recipe (the rub, baste and seasoning) makes for a satisfyingly layered flavour. You'll need a gas or electric barbecue as this joint is cooked slowly.

2.25 to 3.15 kg (5 to 7 lbs) pork shoulder
for mustard baste
235 ml (8 fl oz) spicy mustard
4 tbsp Worcestershire sauce
2 tbsp fresh lemon juice
2 tsp garlic granules
1 tsp onion granules
1 tsp fine ground black pepper
$^1/_2$ tsp cayenne pepper
$^1/_2$ tsp sea salt
for Kansas City rub
4 tbsp granulated sugar

4 tbsp sea salt
2 tbsp brown sugar
4 tsp chilli powder
2 tsp ground cumin
1 tsp cayenne pepper
1 tsp freshly ground black pepper
1 tsp garlic granules
1 tsp onion granules
for finishing pork
120 ml (4 fl oz) apple juice
120 ml (4 fl oz) barbecue sauce
2 tbsp cider vinegar

Trim the excess fat from the pork shoulder. To make the mustard baste, combine all the ingredients in a bowl and blend well. Cover and set aside. To make the rub, combine all the ingredients and blend well. Set aside.

Brush the pork shoulder underside, sides and ends with the mustard baste. Season all over with the rub, reserving 1 tablespoon. Place the pork on the barbecue fat-side up. Cook the butt for 8 hours. Baste every hour with apple juice. Turn the shoulder after 4 hours, and

again after 6 hours. If you are going to slice the butt, cook it to a temperature of 80°C to 85°C (175°F to 185°F). If you want to shred the pork, cook it to a higher temperature of 90°C to 95°C (195°F to 205°F).

If you're slicing the pork, slice and serve with heated barbecue sauce on the side. If pulling the pork, take two large dinner forks and shred the pork, removing any fat. Add the barbecue sauce, cider vinegar and the reserved rub, and blend well. Serve.

Serves 10–12

country-style pork with southern barbecue sauce

see variations page 145

These mouth-watering chunks of pork are deliciously sticky, and make wonderful outdoor finger food.

for the rub
4 tbsp light brown sugar
2 tbsp paprika
1 tbsp garlic granules
1 tbsp chilli powder
1 tbsp onion granules
2 tsp sea salt
2 tsp freshly ground black pepper
1 tsp oregano

1.8 kg (4 lbs) pork shoulder
for the barbecue sauce
225 g (8 oz) jar tomato sauce
5 tbsp black treacle
4 tbsp vinegar
1 tsp garlic granules
1 tsp chilli powder
$\frac{1}{2}$ tsp freshly ground black pepper
2 tsp sea salt

Mix the brown sugar and all the dry spices to make the rub. Cut the pork into 5 cm (2 in) chunks and rub each chunk with the rub on both sides. Set aside to rest. Meanwhile, in a small saucepan, combine the tomato sauce, treacle, vinegar, garlic granules, chilli powder, pepper and salt. Simmer over medium heat for 15 minutes, stirring occasionally.

Preheat the barbecue to medium-hot. Grill the pork for about 20 to 30 minutes or until done, turning as needed to avoid flare-ups and burning. Glaze with the barbecue sauce, and continue to cook until sticky.

Serves 8

barbecued polish pork loin

see variations page 146

Any smoked sausage could be used here, but Polish varieties are especially good.

1.35 to 2.3 kg (3 to 5 lbs) boneless pork loin
15 to 18 cm (6 to 8 in) cooked Polish or
   smoked sausage
4 tbsp vegetable oil
1 medium onion, thinly sliced
for the rub
1 tbsp sugar

1 tsp paprika
1 tsp seasoned salt
1 tsp garlic salt
1 tsp onion salt
1 tsp celery salt
1 tsp dry mustard
1 tsp finely ground black pepper

Mix together the rub ingredients, then set aside. If the loin is rolled, cut the string and unroll. Place the sausage on the loin and re-roll tightly. Tie firmly with string at 2.5 cm (1 in) intervals. Rub the stuffed pork loin with the oil and season it with the rub.

Preheat a covered barbecue or smoker. Place the loin on the grill rack and top with the sliced onion. Cook at 110°C to 120°C (230°F to 250°F), covered, using the indirect method. The loin must reach an internal temperature of 68°C (155°F). Serve carved into thick slices.

Serves 10–12

lamb chops dijon

see variations page 147

A simple but vibrant French-style recipe that brings out the wonderful taste of good lamb chops.

12 lamb loin chops
3 tbsp grated orange zest
3 tbsp chopped fresh thyme

150 ml (5 fl oz) Dijon mustard
2 tbsp light brown sugar
Salt and pepper to taste

Trim any excess fat from the lamb chops. Mix the orange zest and thyme in a bowl. Add the mustard and brown sugar, and stir to combine. Preheat the barbecue.

Brush about half of the mixture onto each side of the chops and place on the hot grill for about 2 minutes per side. Turn the chops over and brush the other half of the mixture onto them. Continue until done. Season with salt and pepper, and serve.

Serves 4

tandoori rack of lamb

see variations page 148

The traditional Indian spice rub on this rack of lamb gives it a fantastic flavour. The lamb is seared hot to seal in the juices and give it a deliciously crusty surface.

$^1/_2$ tsp ground turmeric
$^1/_2$ tsp curry powder
$^1/_2$ tsp ground cumin
$^1/_2$ tsp ground coriander

1 tsp light brown sugar
$^1/_4$ tsp dry mustard
$^1/_4$ tsp ground ginger
One 8-bone rack of lamb

Combine the turmeric, curry powder, cumin, coriander, brown sugar, mustard and ginger. Pat the rack of lamb dry with kitchen paper and coat it with the spice rub. Set aside for 1 hour.

Preheat the grill. Place the lamb on the hot grill rack and sear on each side for about 2 minutes. Reduce the heat or move the lamb to a cooler part of the barbecue and continue grilling until the internal temperature reaches about 54°C (130°F).

Leave to rest for about 10 minutes, then cut the rack into chops and serve.

Serves 8

variations

teriyaki pork burgers

see base recipe page 115

herbed pork burgers

Replace the soy sauce, orange juice, ginger and sugar with 5 tablespoons brandy;
1 tablespoon celery salt; 2 teaspoons each of dried sage and dried rosemary; 1 teaspoon
freshly ground pepper; $\frac{1}{2}$ teaspoon each of dried thyme and crumbled dried summer savory;
$\frac{1}{4}$ teaspoon freshly grated nutmeg; and 1 teaspoon vegetable oil. Proceed with base recipe.

new orleans andouille burgers

Replace the soy sauce, orange juice, ginger and sugar with 2 tablespoons each of paprika,
garlic granules and freshly ground pepper; 1 tablespoon each of sea salt, cayenne pepper,
onion granules, dried oregano and dried thyme; $1\frac{1}{2}$ teaspoons chilli powder; and 1 teaspoon
ground cumin. Proceed with base recipe.

brat burgers

Replace the soy sauce, orange juice, ginger and sugar with 2 teaspoons each of salt, sugar, dry
mustard, paprika, ground coriander, dried sage and freshly ground pepper; and $\frac{1}{4}$ teaspoon
each of dried rosemary, grated nutmeg and cayenne pepper. Proceed with base recipe.

italian burgers

Replace the soy sauce, orange juice, ginger, and sugar with 2 teaspoons garlic granules;
1 teaspoon each of crushed fennel seeds, ground coriander, dried parsley, seasoned salt
and onion granules; $\frac{1}{2}$ teaspoon black pepper; and $\frac{1}{4}$ teaspoon cayenne pepper. Proceed
with base recipe.

variations

jerk barbecued ribs

see base recipe page 116

spice-rubbed ribs
Replace the jerk marinade with a rub made from 55 g (2 oz) light brown sugar; 2 tbsp seasoned salt; 1 teaspoon each of ground allspice, black pepper, ground cumin and ground ginger; and ½ teaspoon ground cinnamon. Proceed with base recipe.

finger-lickin' ribs
Replace jerk marinade with a rub made from 115 g (4 oz) light brown sugar, 2 tablespoons each of seasoned salt, garlic salt, finely ground black pepper and paprika, 1 tablespoon each of onion salt and celery salt, and 1 teaspoon each of dry mustard, onion granules and dried basil. Proceed with base recipe.

zesty no-salt herbal ribs
Replace jerk marinade with a rub made from 115 g (4 oz) granulated sugar; 4 tablespoons chilli powder; 3 tablespoons finely ground black pepper; 1 tablespoon each of chopped fresh dill, garlic granules and onion granules; 2 teaspoons each of celery seeds, chilli powder and lemon juice; and 1 teaspoon each of dried basil, dried marjoram, dry mustard, cayenne pepper, dried parsley, dried rosemary and dried sage. Proceed with base recipe.

carolina-country barbecued ribs
Replace jerk marinade with a marinade made from 235 ml (8 fl oz) cider vinegar; 1 tablespoon each of crushed dried chillies, chopped garlic and sugar; 120 ml (4 fl oz) water; 2 teaspoons dry mustard; and 1 teaspoon each of freshly ground black pepper and dried thyme.

variations

german–style barbecued pork sandwich

see base recipe page 119

bourbon pork tenderloins
Omit the mustard rub. Marinate the pork for 2 hours in a mixture of 175 ml (6 fl oz) soy sauce; 120 ml (4 fl oz) bourbon; 60 ml (2 fl oz) each of Worcestershire sauce, water and vegetable oil; 4 pressed garlic cloves; 3 tablespoons brown sugar; 2 tablespoons freshly ground black pepper; 1 teaspoon salt; and ½ teaspoon ground ginger. Proceed with base recipe.

korean–style pork tenderloins
Omit the mustard rub. Marinate the pork for 2 hours in a mixture of 2 tablespoons sugar, 5 tablespoons soy sauce, 3 tablespoons rice vinegar, 1 tablespoon each of grated ginger and sesame oil, ½ teaspoon crushed dried chillies and 4 pressed garlic cloves. Proceed with base recipe.

pork tenderloins with chilli maple sauce
Omit the mustard rub. Marinate the pork for 2 hours in a mixture of 2 teaspoons ground coriander, 1 teaspoon garlic granules, ½ teaspoon ground ginger, 1 tablespoon vegetable oil and salt and pepper to taste. Serve with a chilli maple sauce: mix 2 tablespoons sherry vinegar, 4 tablespoons maple syrup and 2 teaspoons hot chilli sauce. Proceed with base recipe.

thai tenderloins
Omit the mustard rub. Marinate the pork for 2 hours in a mixture of 60 ml (2 fl oz) fresh orange juice; grated zest of 1 orange; 2 tablespoons fresh coriander; 2 cloves garlic; 3 tablespoons brown sugar; 2 tablespoons each of fresh parsley, soy sauce and peanut butter; 1 tablespoon grated fresh ginger; and 1 teaspoon cayenne pepper. Proceed with base recipe.

variations

black pepper pork steaks with treacle butter

see base recipe page 120

spanish pork steaks

Instead of the treacle butter, marinate the pork steaks for several hours in a mixture of
6 large pressed cloves garlic; 1/4 teaspoon dried oregano; 1/4 teaspoon toasted ground cumin;
120 ml (4 fl oz) orange juice; 2 large onions, thinly sliced; 60 ml (2 fl oz) olive oil; and
120 ml (4 fl oz) dry sherry. Remove the pork steaks and onions from marinade. Grill the
onions alongside the pork.

pork steaks with blue cheese sauce

Instead of treacle butter, make a blue cheese sauce. In a saucepan, stir 2 tablespoons flour
into 4 tablespoons melted sweet butter. Slowly pour in 120 ml (4 fl oz) milk and heat gently
to thicken. Stir in 1 tablespoon chopped fresh parsley; 1 teaspoon garlic granules; 1 teaspoon
sugar; 1 small tomato, peeled, seeded and diced; and 55 g (2 oz) crumbled blue cheese.

bramley apple pork steaks

Instead of serving with treacle butter, make a rub from 1 tablespoon lemon pepper,
1 teaspoon chicken bouillon granules and 1/4 teaspoon ground mace. Serve the grilled pork
steaks with apple sauce.

curry pork steaks

Instead of serving with treacle butter, marinate the chops for 2 hours in a mixture of
60 ml (2 fl oz) soy sauce and 1 tablespoon each of garlic granules, mild curry powder, ground
coriander, cracked black pepper and light brown sugar. Grill as in the base recipe.

variations

st. louis pork steaks

see base recipe page 123

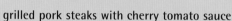

grilled pork steaks with cherry tomato sauce

Omit the vinegar baste and barbecue sauce. Serve the grilled pork with a sauce made by simmering in a saucepan for 10 minutes the following ingredients: one 225 g (8 oz) jar cherry tomato sauce; 1 tablespoon light brown sugar; 2 tablespoons each of Worcestershire sauce, white wine vinegar and tomato purée; 2 red peppers, seeded and chopped; 1 tablespoon onion granules; 1 tablespoon chilli powder; and 1 teaspoon garlic salt.

tangy grilled pork steaks

Omit vinegar baste. Replace the rub with a mixture of 2 tablespoons garlic salt and 1 tablespoon each of onion salt and lemon pepper. For a sauce, stir together 4 tablespoons each of tomato ketchup and Dijon mustard, 2 tablespoons mustard and 2 teaspoons crushed dried chillies.

pork steaks with chilli rub and avocado salsa

Replace the rub and vinegar baste with a rub made from 6 tablespoons chilli powder, 1 tablespoon sugar, 1 tablespoon onion granules and 2 teaspoons each of ground cumin, garlic granules, dried oregano and sea salt. Serve with a salsa made by mixing 475 ml (16 fl oz) tomato and chilli salsa with 2 peeeled, stoned and chopped avocados and 2 tablespoons fresh lime juice.

grilled pork steaks with hoisin glaze

Omit the vinegar baste, rub and barbecue sauce. Serve the grilled pork with a sauce made by combining 120 ml (4 fl oz) hoisin sauce, 1 pressed clove garlic, 1 tablespoon each of cider vinegar and honey, 2 teaspoons grated fresh ginger and a sprinkling of crushed dried chillies.

variations

barbecued pork shoulder

see base recipe page 124

chuckwagon pork shoulder
Replace the Kansas City rub with one made from 1 tablespoon freshly ground black pepper; 2 teaspoons sea salt; 2 teaspoons chilli powder; and 1 teaspoon each of sugar, onion granules, garlic granules, dried parsley and dried oregano.

southern barbecue pork shoulder
Replace the Kansas City rub with one made from 3 tablespoons dried oregano and 2 tablespoons each of garlic granules, freshly ground black pepper, hot chilli powder and salt.

brown sugar pork shoulder
Replace the Kansas City rub with one made from 4 tablespoons brown sugar; 1 tablespoon each of garlic salt, coarse ground black pepper, paprika and chilli powder; 1 teaspoon celery salt; 1/4 teaspoon ground allspice; and 1/4 teaspoon dried thyme.

spicy southeast pork shoulder
Replace the Kansas City rub with one made from 2 tablespoons chilli powder; 1 tablespoon each of paprika, hot paprika, dried oregano, cayenne pepper, garlic granules and sea salt; and 2 teaspoons each of ground cumin, crushed dried chillies and freshly ground black pepper.

variations

country-style pork with southern barbecue sauce

see base recipe page 127

tangy tomato pork

Instead of the rub and sauce, marinate the pork for several hours in the following mixture, puréed in a blender: 120 ml (4 fl oz) red wine vinegar; 235 ml (8 fl oz) olive oil; a 225 g (8 oz) jar tomato sauce; 4 spring onions, chopped; 1 fresh red chilli, seeds and stems removed; 3 tablespoons fresh oregano; 3 cloves garlic, chopped; ½ tablespoon salt; and black pepper to taste.

cider pork

Instead of the rub, marinate the pork in the following mixture: 2 tablespoons onion granules; 1 tablespoon each of sea salt, coarse ground black pepper and garlic granules; 475 ml (16 fl oz) each of cider vinegar and cider; 115 g (4 oz) light brown sugar; 4 tablespoons Worcestershire sauce; and 2 tablespoons crushed dried chillies.

char siu chinese barbecued pork

Instead of the rub and sauce, make a glaze by mixing together 4 tablespoons hoisin sauce; 2 tablespoons each chicken stock, Chinese rice wine and soy sauce; 1 pressed clove garlic; 1½ tablespoons honey; ¾ teaspoon sea salt; and a few drops of red food colouring.

country pork with apricot glaze

Instead of the rub and sauce, make a glaze by mixing together 3 tablespoons apricot conserve, 1 tablespoon tomato ketchup, 2 seeded and chopped red chillies and 1 teaspoon ground cumin. Simmer together for 15 minutes and brush over the pork while grilling.

variations

barbecued polish pork loin

see base recipe page 128

tex-mex country pork loin
Omit the sausage and replace the rub with a mixture of 2 tablespoons light brown sugar;
1 tablespoon garlic granules; and 2 teaspoons each of ground cumin, chilli powder, onion
granules, freshly ground black pepper and paprika. Proceed with base recipe.

bacon-wrapped barbecued pork loin
Omit the sausage and wrap the loin with 225 g (8 oz) streaky bacon rashers. Replace the
rub with a mixture of 115 g (4 oz) dark brown sugar; 4 tablespoons paprika; 2 tablespoons
seasoned salt; 1 tablespoon each of black pepper, white pepper, cayenne pepper, garlic salt,
onion salt and dry mustard; and 2 teaspoons dried sage. Proceed with base recipe.

gourmet pepper-crusted barbecued pork loin
Omit the sausage and replace the rub with a mixture of 4 tablespoons coarsely ground mixed
peppercorns; 4 tablespoons light brown sugar; 2 tablespoons each of dry mustard, celery salt
and garlic salt; and 1 teaspoon chilli powder. Proceed with base recipe.

elegant barbecued pork loin
Omit everything except the pork loin. Brush the pork loin with 120 ml (4 fl oz) balsamic
vinegar. Combine 2 tablespoons each of garlic salt and coarse ground black pepper and
1 tablespoon chopped fresh rosemary. Sprinkle this mixture over the loin before cooking.
Proceed with base recipe.

lamb chops dijon

see base recipe page 131

armenian lamb chops
Replace the mustard glaze with a marinade: 1 finely chopped onion, 120 ml (4 fl oz) red wine, 3 tablespoons chopped flat-leaf parsley and 2 teaspoons each chopped fresh mint and fresh basil. Marinate the chops for 2 hours. Proceed with base recipe.

grilled ginger and red wine lamb chops
Replace the mustard glaze with a marinade: mix together 3 tablespoons olive oil; 2 tablespoons each of red wine and soy sauce; 2 cloves pressed garlic; 1 tablespoon each lemon juice and grated fresh ginger; 1½ teaspoons onion granules; ¼ teaspoon cayenne pepper and 3 to 4 tablespoons lukewarm water. Marinate the chops for 2 hours. Proceed with base recipe.

apple-glazed lamb chops
Replace the mustard glaze with an apple glaze: heat 120 ml (4 fl oz) apple sauce, 4 tablespoons lemon juice and 60 ml (2 fl oz) steak sauce gently in a saucepan. Add salt and pepper to taste, and glaze the chops before grilling as directed. Proceed with base recipe.

chilli-rubbed lamb chops
Replace the mustard glaze with a chilli rub. Mix together 1½ tablespoons chilli powder; 2 teaspoons ground cumin; 1 teaspoon each of dried thyme, sugar and freshly ground black pepper; ¾ teaspoon salt, and ¼ teaspoon ground allspice. Proceed with base recipe. Serve the grilled chops with redcurrant jelly.

variations

tandoori rack of lamb

see base recipe page 132

arizona rack of lamb
Replace the spice rub with: 115 g (4 oz) unsalted butter, softened; 2 teaspoons each of chilli powder and paprika; 1 teaspoon ground cumin and garlic granules; ½ teaspoon each of onion powder, smoked paprika, oregano and freshly ground black pepper. Proceed with base recipe.

curried rack of lamb
Replace the spice rub with: 2 tablespoons sea salt; 1 tablespoon curry powder; 2 teaspoons onion powder, 1 teaspoon each of freshly ground black pepper, garlic granules and chilli powder and ½ teaspoon ground allspice. Proceed with base recipe.

marinated rack of lamb with orange marmalade glaze
Omit spice rub. Combine 235 ml (8 fl oz) olive oil; 2 tablespoons garlic salt; 1 teaspoon each of dried thyme, dried rosemary and freshly ground black pepper. Marinate lamb for 2 hours. Combine 235 ml (8 fl oz) orange marmalade, 120 ml (4 fl oz) fresh orange juice, 2 tablespoons fresh lemon juice, 1 tablespoon triple sec and ⅛ teaspoon each of sea salt and white pepper. Purée. Heat in a saucepan, adding 2 tablespoons unsalted butter. Use this mixture to glaze the marinated lamb as it cooks.

honey glazed rack of lamb
Replace the spice rub with 2 tablespoons lemon pepper and 1 tablespoon garlic salt. Combine in a small bowl 3 tablespoons each of honey, fresh lemon juice and soy sauce; and 2 cloves garlic, crushed. Use this mixture to glaze the lamb as it cooks.

spicy rotisserie leg of lamb

see base recipe page 135

garlic-dijon leg of lamb
Omit everything except the lamb. Make a mustard marinade: combine 120 ml (4 fl oz) Dijon mustard; 4 large cloves garlic, each sliced into 4 thin slivers; 2 tablespoons onion salt and 1 tablespoon freshly ground black pepper. Proceed with base recipe.

balsamic vinegar and rosemary leg of lamb
Omit everything except the lamb. Mix 60 ml (2 fl oz) balsamic vinegar, 2 tablespoons honey, 2 teaspoons each of olive oil, dried rosemary and garlic granules; and 1 teaspoon each of sea salt and freshly ground black pepper. Proceed with base recipe. Brush over the lamb before barbecuing

greek-flavoured leg of lamb
Omit everything except the lamb. Mix 60 ml (2 fl oz) Worcestershire sauce; 2 teaspoons dried oregano; 1½ teaspoons onion powder; 1½ teaspoons garlic granules; 1 teaspoon each of sea salt, freshly ground black pepper, beef bouillon granules and dried parsley; and ½ teaspoon ground cinnamon and ground nutmeg. Proceed with base recipe. Rub over the lamb before barbecuing.

classic leg of lamb
Omit everything except the lamb. Mix 60 ml (2 fl oz) extra-virgin olive oil, 2 tablespoons sea salt and 1 tablespoon each of freshly ground black pepper, garlic granules and dried rosemary. Proceed with base recipe. Rub into the lamb before barbecuing.

variations

grilled denver lamb ribs

see base recipe page 136

lamb ribs provençal
Replace the marinade with a herb rub. Mix together 1 tablespoon dried parsley, 2 teaspoons each of garlic granules, onion powder and *herbes de Provence*, and 1 teaspoon each of freshly ground black pepper, sea salt and olive oil.

spiced lamb riblets
Replace the marinade with: 235 ml (8 fl oz) plain low-fat yoghurt, 2 tablespoons spicy mustard, 2 large crushed cloves garlic, 1 tablespoon each of soy sauce and fresh lemon juice and 1 teaspoon cayenne pepper.

barbecued lamb ribs
Replace the marinade with: 475 ml (16 fl oz) barbecue sauce; 120 ml (4 fl oz) white wine; 2 tablespoons oil; 1 tablespoon sugar; 1 lemon, thinly sliced; ½ teaspoon each of crushed peppercorns, fresh thyme and crushed juniper berries; 1 teaspoon salt.

spicy barbecue colorado lamb ribs
Replace the marinade with 120 ml (4 fl oz) cider; 1 tablespoon grated fresh ginger; and 2 tablespoons each of vegetable oil, soy sauce and clear honey. Make a spicy barbecue sauce to serve with the ribs by combining in a saucepan 235 ml (8 fl oz) each of tomato paste and cider vinegar, 120 ml (4 fl oz) each of black treacle and packed brown sugar, 60 ml (2 fl oz) each of soy sauce and Worcestershire sauce, 2 tablespoons yellow mustard, 1 teaspoon each of sea salt and black pepper, and ½ teaspoon cayenne pepper.

barbecued texas cabrito

see base recipe page 138

jerked cabrito

Replace the rub with a mixture of: 2 onions, grated; 120 ml (4 fl oz) soy sauce; 6 large crushed cloves garlic; 1 tablespoon each of chopped fresh thyme leaves, ground allspice and sea salt; 2 teaspoons freshly ground black pepper; 1 teaspoon ground cinnamon; ½ teaspoon ground nutmeg and 1 fresh red chilli, seeded and finely chopped. Reduce the baste ingredients to one 355 ml (12 fl oz) can beer and 60 ml (2 fl oz) fresh lemon juice.

kansas city cabrito

Replace the rub with a mixture of: 2 tablespoons sea salt and 1 tablespoon each of freshly ground black pepper, garlic granules, onion powder, ground cumin and cayenne pepper. Reduce the baste ingredients to one 355 ml (12 fl oz) can beer and 60 ml (2 fl oz) fresh lemon juice.

barbecued cabrito

Replace the rub with a mixture of 3 tablespoons salt and pepper and 1 tablespoon paprika. Alter the baste recipe to: 5 crushed cloves garlic, 120 ml (4 fl oz) each of vegetable oil and cider vinegar, 60 ml (2 fl oz) water, 2 tablespoons Worcestershire sauce, 2 bay leaves and 2 halved and juiced lemons.

cooper's cabrito

Replace the rub with a mixture of 3 tablespoons freshly ground black pepper, 2 tablespoons sea salt and 2 teaspoons cayenne pepper.

succulent beef

Nothing brings out the natural flavours of beef better than the grill. Whether you're in the mood for a simple steak or want to go all out with a succulent prime rib, there's something here to satisfy your beef craving.

beef brisket with spicy rub

see variations page 180

Served with an angel's mustard slather, this is melt-in-the-mouth tender and tasty.

2 tsp garlic granules
1 tsp onion granules
$1/2$ tsp cayenne pepper, freshly ground
1 tsp black pepper, freshly ground
$1/2$ tsp white pepper
$1/2$ tsp sea salt
2 tbsp soy sauce
2 tbsp white wine
2 tbsp Worcestershire sauce
235 ml (8 fl oz) Dijon or yellow mustard
200 g (8 oz) granulated sugar

1 tbsp seasoned salt
1 tbsp garlic salt
1 tbsp onion salt
1 tbsp celery salt
2 tbsp paprika
1 tbsp chilli powder
1 tsp ground ginger
1 tsp mild chilli powder
$1/2$ tsp ground allspice
$1/2$ tsp ground dry mustard
One 1.8 to 3.6 kg (4 to 8 lb) brisket joint

To make the mustard slather, put the garlic granules, onion granules, cayenne pepper, peppers and salt in a bowl. Blend in the soy sauce, white wine and Worcestershire sauce and stir with a whisk to mix the spices well, then stir in the mustard. Cover and set aside. Combine the remaining dry seasonings and blend well to make a rub. Set aside. Trim most of the fat from the brisket, leaving a 3 to 5 mm ($1/4$ to $1/8$ in) thin layer. Using a pastry brush, cover the lean side of the brisket with the mustard slather. Sprinkle on the rub. Turn the brisket over and repeat the process on the fat side. Don't forget to season the ends and sides. Preheat a covered barbecue or smoker. Place the brisket on your grill and smoke for 8 to 12 hours or until a skewer inserted in the flat part of the brisket, against the grain, goes in and comes out with no resistance.

Serves 8

carne asada

see variations page 181

This Mexican classic is perfect for outdoor eating on lazy summer evenings.

120 ml (4 fl oz) tequila
4 tbsp fresh lime juice
4 tbsp fresh lemon juice
4 tbsp fresh orange juice
4 cloves garlic, crushed
1 onion, grated
Tabasco sauce to taste

1 tsp freshly ground black pepper
900 g (2 lb) flank or top rump
12 flour tortillas
235 ml (8 fl oz) salsa
235 ml (8 fl oz) guacamole
Tabasco or taco sauce to taste

Mix the tequila, citrus juices, garlic, onion, Tabasco and pepper in a bowl. Reserve 60 ml (2 fl oz) of the marinade. Add the beef to the remaining marinade, cover the bowl and marinate for 4 hours or (for better results) overnight. Turn occasionally while marinating.

Preheat a grill to medium. Place a few drops of water on each tortilla, stack and wrap in heavy-duty aluminium foil. Place on the grill. Remove the beef from the bowl and discard the marinade. Place the steak on the grill. Turn the meat and tortillas once during cooking, and brush the beef with the reserved marinade. Cook to your liking (12 to 15 minutes for medium-rare). Cut the beef into thin slices across the grain. Place a few slices of beef on each tortilla with salsa and guacamole, and serve with Tabasco or taco sauce.

Serves 6

barbecued t-bone steak

see variations page 182

T-bone steaks have both fillet and sirloin together, making them especially tasty and tender.

Two 4 cm (1½ in) T-bone steaks, 900 g (2 lbs) each
1 tbsp coarse sea salt
1 tbsp coarsely ground black pepper

2 tbsp unsalted butter
235 ml (8 fl oz) flat pale ale
2 tbsp Worcestershire sauce

Generously sprinkle the steaks with salt and pepper and set them aside, covered, at room temperature for 30 to 45 minutes. Melt the butter in a small saucepan over medium heat. Remove the pan from the heat, stir in the ale and Worcestershire sauce and reserve the mixture. Prepare the grill for a two-level fire capable of cooking first on high heat and then on medium heat.

Keeping the smaller, more tender sections angled away from the hottest part of the grill, grill the steaks, uncovered, for 2½ to 3 minutes per side. Move the steaks to medium heat, turning them again, and continue grilling for 3 to 4 minutes per side for the medium-rare doneness. Steaks should be turned a minimum of three times (more often if juice begins to form on the surface). If grilling covered, sear both sides of the meat first on high heat, uncovered, for 2½ to 3 minutes; finish cooking, covered, over medium heat for 5 to 7 minutes, turning the steaks once halfway through. Transfer the steaks to a serving platter and immediately top with equal amounts of the beer-butter mixture. At the table, slice the steaks from the bones in thin strips and serve hot, making sure to spoon meat juices and beer-butter on each portion.

Serves 4-6

the ultimate steakhouse burger

see variations page 183

A classic burger, stripped back to its basics and unadulterated by extra flavourings.

8 bacon rashers
3 slices fresh Italian bread without crust or
   sesame seeds, cubed
4 tbsp whole milk
680 g (1½ lbs) lean minced beef

1 tsp sea salt
1 tsp freshly ground black pepper or to taste
2 large cloves garlic, crushed
Garnish: sliced tomatoes, onions, lettuce leaves

Fry the bacon in a large frying pan over medium heat until crisp. Drain on paper towels. Spoon 3 tablespoons of the bacon fat into a heatproof bowl and refrigerate while preparing the other ingredients. Place the bread into a small bowl, add the milk and leave until the bread is saturated, about 5 minutes. Using a fork, mash the bread and milk to a smooth paste. Break the beef into small pieces in a medium bowl, then add the salt and pepper with the garlic, bread paste and reserved bacon fat. With your hands, lightly knead together so the mixture forms a cohesive mass.

Divide the meat mixture into 4 equal patties about 2 cm (¾ in) thick. Grill over a high heat on a preheated grill for that charred flavour, until both sides are seared. Allow 4 to 5 minutes per side for medium rare, or longer if desired. Do not press down on the burgers as they cook. Serve with the bacon, sliced tomatoes, onions, lettuce leaves or any other garnish you choose.

Serves 4

beer-marinated peppered t-bones

see variations page 184

Marinating the steaks in beer tenderises them as well as adding extra flavour.

1 onion, grated
175 ml (6 fl oz) flat beer
175 ml (6 fl oz) bottled chilli sauce
2 tbsp chopped fresh parsley
3 tbsp Dijon-style mustard
1 tbsp Worcestershire sauce
1 tbsp light brown sugar

1 tsp paprika
$\frac{1}{2}$ tsp freshly ground black pepper
Four 340- to 455-g (12- to 16-oz) T-bone
    steaks
1 tbsp sea salt or to taste
1 tbsp cracked black pepper or to taste
Fresh herbs (optional)

In a small bowl combine the onion, beer, chilli sauce, parsley, mustard, Worcestershire sauce, brown sugar, paprika and $\frac{1}{2}$ teaspoon black pepper. Place the steaks in the marinade. Cover and refrigerate 4 to 6 hours or overnight, turning the steaks over occasionally.

Remove the steaks from the marinade; discard the marinade. Sprinkle both sides of steaks with sea salt and the cracked black pepper.

Preheat the barbecue. Grill steaks on an uncovered grill directly over medium heat for 5 to 7 minutes. Turn and grill to the desired doneness, allowing 7 to 10 minutes more for medium-rare doneness. If desired, garnish with roughly chopped fresh herbs.

Serves 4

grilled marinated sirloin steak

see variations page 185

The simple flavours of this marinade do not interfere with the fine taste of the steak.

One 225-g (8-oz) sirloin steak, cut
    2.5-cm (1-in) thick and well trimmed
4 tbsp balsamic vinegar
2 tbsp tomato paste
2 large cloves garlic, crushed

1 tbsp fresh thyme leaves
1 tbsp fresh marjoram leaves
1 tbsp sea salt or to taste
1 tsp freshly ground black pepper

Place the steak in a shallow glass dish or pie dish. Combine the remaining ingredients; spread evenly over both sides of the steak. Leave to stand at room temperature for 30 minutes, or cover and refrigerate for up to 8 hours. Remove the steak from its marinade; discard the marinade.

Preheat a grill to medium. Grill the steak 10 to 13 cm (4 to 5 in) from the heat source, for 4 minutes per side for medium-rare, or to desired doneness.

Slice the steak into thin strips and serve immediately.

Serves 4

balsamic rump steaks

see variations page 186

Marinate rump steaks to tenderise them, then cook them quickly and serve rare or medium-rare.

575 ml (1 pt) balsamic vinegar
120 ml (4 fl oz) Worcestershire sauce
200 g (7 oz) light brown sugar
1 tbsp salt
Four 175 g- to 225-g (6- to 8-oz) rump steaks
Salt and pepper to taste

Combine 475 ml (16 fl oz) of balsamic vinegar with the Worcestershire sauce, brown sugar and 1 tablespoon salt. Mix until the sugar is dissolved. Place the steaks in a large resealable polythene bag. Pour the marinade over the steaks, seal the bag and turn to coat. Marinate the steaks for 3 to 4 hours. Meanwhile place the remaining balsamic vinegar in a saucepan. Bring to the boil and reduce by half. Set aside and leave to cool. It will continue to thicken as it cools.

Preheat the barbecue. Remove the steaks from their marinade and discard the marinade. Season with salt and pepper. Place on a grill preheated to high. Grill over a high heat for about 3 minutes per side, brushing each side regularly with the thickened balsamic vinegar while cooking. Grill until rare or medium-rare, remove from the grill and serve. Cut each steak on the bias into thin slices. Fan out the slices on warm dinner plates.

Serves 4

fillet steaks with herbed cheese

see variations page 187

Beef fillet is an excellent cut for barbecues because it remains meltingly tender when grilled.

2 tbsp softened cream cheese
2 tbsp blue cheese, crumbled
1 tbsp plain yoghurt
1 tbsp grated onion
2 tsp freshly ground black pepper
Four 225-g (8-oz) beef tenderloin steaks

1 large garlic clove, halved
Cooking spray
1 tsp sea salt or to taste
1 tsp freshly ground black pepper
2 tsp chopped fresh parsley

Combine the cream cheese, blue cheese, yoghurt, onion and pepper; reserve. Rub each side of the beef steaks with the garlic. Spray the steaks with cooking spray and season all over with salt and pepper to taste.

Preheat the barbecue. Grill the steaks on medium heat for 5 to 6 minutes. Turn and grill for 3 to 4 minutes more. Top each steak with an equal amount of the cheese mixture. Grill for an additional 1 to 2 minutes. Garnish with parsley and serve hot.

Serves 4

grilled top rump with aïoli

see variations page 188

Aïoli, a rich and flavoursome garlic mayonnaise from Provence, is the perfect partner for steak.

680 g (1½ lbs) top rump or thick flank,
    trimmed of any sinew
120 ml (4 fl oz) red wine vinegar
2 cloves garlic, crushed
2 tbsp olive oil
Cooking spray

for the aïoli
7 large cloves garlic
2 large egg yolks
2 tbsp sherry vinegar
120 ml (4 fl oz) extra-virgin olive oil
Sea salt and freshly ground black pepper

Place the beef in a resealable polythene bag with the vinegar, garlic and 2 tablespoons oil; shake to coat thoroughly. Leave to marinate in the refrigerator for 4 to 8 hours or overnight.

Place the garlic and egg yolks in a blender or food processor and pulse until the garlic is finely chopped. Add the vinegar and blend. With the blender or food processor running, slowly add the olive oil in a thin stream until the mixture thickens. Remove to a bowl and season to taste. Immediately refrigerate until ready for use.

Preheat the barbecue. Remove the beef from the marinade and discard the marinade. Spray the beef with cooking spray and grill over medium heat for about 4 to 6 minutes on each side or until medium-rare. Remove from the grill and leave to rest for about 5 minutes. Slice the beef across the grain and serve at once with the aïoli on the side in small ramekins.

Serves 4

béarnaise butter

see variations page 189

This is the classic French accompaniment for a simply grilled steak.

3 shallots, finely chopped
4 tbsp wine vinegar
4 tbsp white wine
1 tsp dried tarragon

225 g (8 oz) unsalted butter, softened
$1/2$ tsp sea salt
1 tsp dried parsley

In a small pan, combine the shallots, wine vinegar, wine and tarragon. Bring to the boil and reduce to a thick glaze. Cool. Add this to the butter and season with the parsley and salt, blending until well incorporated. Place the butter mixture in the middle of a sheet of cling film and form into a cylinder. Chill or freeze.

Slice off pieces just prior to taking the steak off the grill. Place them on the steak during the resting period and they will melt beautifully over the top of the steak. Depending on how big your roll is, 5 mm- ($1/4$ in-) thick slices are usually appropriate.

Serves 4

simply grilled sirloin

see variations page 190

The simplest seasonings are often the best, allowing the flavours of top-quality steaks to speak for themselves.

4 sirloin steaks, 2.5-cm (1-in.) thick
1 tbsp sea salt
1 tbsp freshly ground black pepper

Season the steaks all over with the salt and pepper to taste. Leave the steaks to rest, covered, for 30 minutes at room temperature.

Preheat the barbecue. Grill over high heat on a preheated grill for 8 to 10 minutes per side for medium-rare, or longer if desired. Rotate the steaks a quarter turn after the first 2½ minutes on the grill to create crisscrossed grill marks. Remove from the grill, loosely cover with aluminium foil and leave to rest for about 10 minutes before serving.

Serves 4

barbecued beef rib racks

see variations page 191

Beef back ribs are incredibly succulent and flavoursome. To serve, just cut down between the ribs.

for the dry rub
2 tbsp freshly ground black pepper
1 tbsp garlic salt
1 tbsp onion salt
1 tbsp sweet paprika
1 tsp cayenne pepper or to taste
Four 175- to 225-g (6- to 8-oz) beef back
    rib racks

for the mopping sauce
60 ml (2 fl oz) vegetable oil
60 ml (2 fl oz) fresh lemon juice
2 tbsp ketchup
1 tsp freshly ground black pepper
1 tsp dry mustard

Combine the dry rub ingredients and blend well. Season the rib racks on both sides with the rub. Combine all the ingredients in the small saucepan for the mopping sauce. Heat for 10 minutes over medium or low heat.

Cook the rib racks using the indirect method between 110°C and 120°C (230°F and 250°F) for about 2 to 4 hours, depending on the size of the ribs. Turn the ribs after cooking for 2 hours and brush with a light coat of the mopping sauce. Cook until the ribs are tender, brushing them occasionally with the mopping sauce. The ribs are done when they are pierced easily with a knife.

Serves 4

devilled chuck steak

see variations page 192

Chuck steak needs slow and careful cooking, but the overnight marinating involved here will help to tenderise it beautifully.

Two 450- to 675-g (1- to 1½-lb) slices chuck
   or braising steak (about 2-cm (¾-in) thick)
Unseasoned meat tenderiser
235 ml (8 fl oz) beef stock
55 g (2 oz) light brown sugar
2 tbsp fresh lemon juice
2 tbsp Worcestershire sauce

2 tbsp yellow mustard
1 tsp garlic granules
1 tsp freshly ground black pepper
½ tsp curry powder
½ tsp cayenne pepper
¼ tsp ground bay leaf

Trim any excess fat from the chuck steaks. Prepare the steak with meat tenderiser following the package instructions, cover and place in the refrigerator for about an hour. Mix the rest of the ingredients in a bowl; set aside. Place the steaks in a large resealable polythene bag and pour ¾ of the marinade over. Seal and leave to marinate for 4 to 6 hours or overnight in the refrigerator.

Preheat the barbecue. Remove the steak from the marinade and discard the marinade. Place the steak on a preheated grill over medium heat; grill for 35 minutes for rare or until it reaches desired doneness, turning the steak occasionally. Baste regularly with the remaining marinade. Remove the steak from the grill, cover loosely with aluminium foil and set aside for 5 to 10 minutes, before serving.

Serves 4-6

argentinian-style rib eye steaks

see variations page 193

No one cooks beef as well as the Argentinians, and this method is particularly successful.

4 rib eye steaks cut 2.5-cm (1-in) thick
1 tsp sea salt or to taste
1 tsp freshly ground black pepper or to taste
3 tbsp olive oil
3 tbsp chopped fresh flat-leaf parsley

1 tbsp finely chopped fresh oregano
3 or 4 cloves garlic, finely chopped
1 tsp cayenne pepper

Season the steaks all over with salt and pepper to taste. Preheat the barbecue, then grill the steaks, uncovered, directly over medium heat to desired doneness, turning once. Allow 8 to 10 minutes for medium-rare doneness or 12 to 15 minutes for medium doneness.

Meanwhile, to make the sauce, stir together the olive oil, parsley, oregano, garlic, salt and cayenne pepper. Spoon the sauce on top of the steaks for the last 2 minutes of grilling.

Serves 4

grilled chilean skirt steak

see variations page 194

Skirt steak is a tasty cut, and the haunting flavour of this Chilean rub makes it even more appetising. Use thick flank or top rump if you prefer.

900-g (2-lb) skirt steak
235 ml (8 fl oz) fresh lime juice (about 8 limes)
for the rub
2 tbsp ground toasted cumin
1 tbsp garlic granules
4 tbsp dried coriander leaves, crushed
Sea salt and freshly ground black pepper
    to taste

for the relish
75 g (3 oz) finely chopped pitted green olives
1 tsp crushed dried chillies, or to taste
4 tbsp olive oil
2 tbsp freshly ground black pepper

Place the steak in a resealable polythene bag or shallow dish and pour the lime juice over it. Seal the bag or cover the dish the dish and let it sit in the refrigerator for 30 minutes to 1 hour, turning occasionally. In a small bowl, combine all the rub ingredients and mix well. Remove the steak from the marinade, pat dry with paper towels and rub it all over with the spice rub, pressing gently to be sure it sticks. Preheat the barbecue, then grill over medium heat for 4 to 5 minutes per side for medium-rare.

Remove the steak from the heat, cover it loosely with foil and leave it to rest for 5 minutes while you make the relish. In a medium bowl, combine all the relish ingredients and mix well. Slice the steak as thin as possible against the grain on a bias. Serve with the relish, warm flour tortillas, rice and beans.

Serves 6

grilled veal chops with rosemary

see variations page 195

Veal cooked with wine and rosemary unites some of the classic flavours of Tuscany – and the aroma while it grills is sensational.

120 ml (4 fl oz) olive oil
60 ml (2 fl oz) dry red wine
1¹/₂ tbsp chopped fresh rosemary
4 large cloves garlic, crushed
¹/₂ tsp sea salt
¹/₂ tsp freshly ground black pepper
Six 225 g (8-oz) veal rib chops, 2- to 2.5-cm
    (³/₄- to 1-in thick)
Fresh rosemary sprigs

Whisk the oil, wine, rosemary, garlic, salt and pepper to blend in a glass dish. Add the veal chops to the dish and turn to coat with the marinade. Leave to stand at room temperature for 1 hour or refrigerate for up to 4 hours, turning the veal occasionally.

Preheat the barbecue grill to medium. Remove the veal from its marinade, shaking off the excess. Season the veal chops with salt and pepper. Grill the veal until cooked to your desired doneness, turning once and allowing about 4 minutes per side for medium-rare. Transfer to a platter. Garnish with fresh rosemary sprigs and serve.

Serves 6

barbecued beef ribs

see variations page 196

The rub used for cooking these beef ribs is mouthwateringly savoury – you'll want to eat them all.

3 tbsp sea salt
$^{1}/_{4}$ tsp cayenne pepper
$^{1}/_{2}$ tsp black pepper
$^{1}/_{2}$ tsp garlic granules
$^{1}/_{2}$ tsp onion granules

$^{1}/_{2}$ tsp paprika
$^{1}/_{2}$ tsp ground cumin
1.8 kg (4 lbs) beef back ribs
Prepared barbecue sauce for basting

Combine all the ingredients except the ribs and barbecue sauce in a small bowl, mixing well. Wash the ribs and pat them dry. Rub with seasoning mixture and store the remainder. Place a disposable foil drip pan under the grates of the barbecue and wipe the grates with oil to prevent sticking. Preheat the grill to high. Place the ribs over the drip pan, cover and reduce the heat to low. Baste the ribs at the end of the cooking process with the sauce of your choice. Baste once 20 minutes before ribs are done, and a second time 10 minutes later.

Average-size ribs are cooked rare in 25–30 minutes, medium-rare in 35–40 minutes and well done in 45–50 minutes. These times will vary according to the grill used and the size of the ribs. Small ribs may require less cooking time, while large ribs may need a little more time on the grill. Adjust accordingly.

Serves 4

grilled sirloin roast

see variations page 197

Sirloin is one of the best joints for barbecues because of its full flavour and lack of fat. Try preparing it with this basic rub for a sensational yet simple grilled feast.

1 tbsp garlic granules
1 tbsp onion granules
1 tbsp paprika
1 tbsp coarse ground black pepper
1 tbsp sea salt
1.35- to 1.8-kg (3- to 4-lb) sirloin joint

Combine all the ingredients except the tri-tip and blend well. Lightly oil the cooking grate on your grill. Preheat the grill and prepare for indirect grilling or direct grilling. Combine the garlic granules, onion granules, paprika, pepper and salt. Rub it over the surface of the sirloin roast. Place the sirloin on the grill, fat side up. You could place a metal drip pan under it to catch the juices, which will make a delicious gravy later.

With the grill on low, cook for about 4 hours or until the internal temperature reaches 63°C (145°F) for medium-rare, or up to 75°C (165°F) for medium-well. If you are going to grill directly, cook the sirloin, covered, over a medium heat, turning every 15 to 20 minutes, until the meat reaches the desired temperature.

Serves 4

variations

beef brisket with spicy rub

see base recipe page 153

jack's brisket rub
Replace the spicy rub with a rub made from 4 tablespoons salt; 2 tablespoons each of granulated and light brown sugar; 2 teaspoons each of dry mustard, onion granules, garlic granules and dried basil; 1 teaspoon black pepper; ³⁄₄ teaspoon dried coriander; ¹⁄₂ teaspoon dried savory; and ¹⁄₂ teaspoon ground cumin. Proceed with base recipe.

texas brisket rub
Replace the spicy rub with a rub made from 4 tablespoons coarsely ground black pepper, 3 tablespoons sea salt, 2 tablespoons paprika and 1 tablespoon cayenne pepper. Proceed with base recipe.

spicy kansas city brisket rub
Replace the spicy rub with a rub made from 4 tablespoons paprika; 2 tablespoons chilli powder; 1 tablespoon each of ground black pepper, ground white pepper, granulated sugar, ground cumin, garlic granules, light brown sugar, dried oregano and celery salt; 2 teaspoons cayenne pepper; and 1 teaspoon dry mustard. Proceed with base recipe.

stu carpenter's brisket rub
Replace the spicy rub with a rub made from 2 tablespoons each of freshly ground black pepper, light brown sugar and paprika; 1 tablespoon sea salt; 2 teaspoons garlic granules; 1 teaspoon each of chilli powder, onion granules, ground cumin and granulated sugar; and ¹⁄₂ teaspoon each of dry mustard and mild chilli powder. Proceed with base recipe.

variations

carne asada

see base recipe page 154

manuel's fajitas
Replace the marinade with one made by combining 120 ml (4 fl oz) soy sauce, 120 ml (4 fl oz) fresh lemon juice, 225 g (8 oz) light brown sugar and 1 tablespoon each of onion granules, garlic granules and ground ginger. Wrap slices of grilled meat inside each tortilla.

west texas grilled fajitas
Replace the marinade with one made by combining 120 ml (4 fl oz) fresh lime juice; 60 ml (2 fl oz) red wine vinegar; 2 tablespoons each of soy sauce, chilli powder, ground cumin, light molasses and chopped coriander; 4 large garlic cloves, crushed; and 1 teaspoon ground pepper. Wrap slices of grilled meat inside each tortilla.

bichelmeyer's meat market fajitas
Replace the marinade with one made by combining 4 large garlic cloves, crushed; 1 fresh red chilli pepper, seeded and finely chopped; 120 ml (4 fl oz) vegetable oil; 60 ml (2 fl oz) each of fresh lime juice and cider vinegar; and 1 tablespoon sugar. Wrap slices of grilled meat inside each tortilla.

spiky lime carne asada
Replace the marinade with one made by combining 235 ml (8 fl oz) lime juice, 120 ml (4 fl oz) olive oil and a small bunch of fresh coriander (leaves and stalks), chopped. Wrap slices of grilled meat inside each tortilla.

variations

barbecued t-bone steak

see base recipe page 157

t-bone steaks with mushroom and garlic sauce

Replace the beer-butter mixture with a mushroom and garlic sauce. Make this by sautéing in a frying pan 455 g (1 lb) sliced mushrooms, 3 crushed large garlic cloves and 1 tablespoon vegetable oil until the mushrooms are soft. Whisk in 3 tablespoons butter, 3 tablespoons flour and 355 ml (12 fl oz) beef broth. Proceed with base recipe.

southern grilled garlic t-bone steaks

Replace the beer-butter mixture with a marinade made by mixing together 235 ml (8 fl oz) Italian salad dressing, 235 ml (8 fl oz) barbecue sauce, 120 ml (4 fl oz) Worcestershire sauce and 2 large, crushed garlic cloves. Marinate the steaks for 2 hours. Proceed with base recipe.

marinated grilled t-bone steaks

Replace the beer-butter mixture with a marinade made by mixing together 60 ml (2 fl oz) olive oil; 2 tablespoons each of crushed fresh garlic, balsamic vinegar and fresh lemon juice; and the finely chopped leaves of 1 fresh rosemary sprig. Marinate the steaks for 2 hours. Proceed with base recipe.

t-bone steaks with bourbon and shallot sauce

Replace the beer-butter mixture with a marinade made by mixing together 120 ml (4 fl oz) honey mustard, 120 ml (4 fl oz) bourbon, 2 finely chopped shallots and salt to taste. Marinate the steaks for 2 hours. Proceed with base recipe.

the ultimate steakhouse burger

see base recipe page 158

hamburgers with 'hot' barbecue sauce
Make a sauce for the burgers by simmering together for 10 minutes the following
ingredients: 235 ml (8 fl oz) ketchup; 4 tablespoons white vinegar; 3 tablespoons each of
Worcestershire sauce and light brown sugar; and 2 tablespoons each of water and prepared
horseradish. Mix well and serve warm.

healthy grilled burgers
Omit the burger ingredients and bacon slices. Replace with a mixture of 225 g (8 oz)
each of minced turkey thigh meat, dried breadcrumbs, silken tofu and grated carrots; a
handful of chopped watercress; 1 small onion, finely chopped; and salt and pepper to taste.

new mexico green chilli burgers
Omit garnishes. Instead, garnish each burger with sliced Cheddar cheese, bottled green
chillies, sliced red onion, sliced tomato, shredded romaine leaves and fresh salsa.

french bistro burger
Omit the bacon slices and other garnishes. Top the burger with walnuts, Gruyère cheese
and garlic and mustard mayonnaise. Serve on a French roll.

the ultimate lamb burger
Omit the bacon and garlic. Replace the minced beef with lean minced lamb and
1½ teaspoons dried mint. Garnish as in base recipe.

variations

beer-marinated peppered t-bones

see base recipe page 161

grilled t-bones with cowboy grilled onions
Omit the marinade. Serve the grilled steaks topped with 4 sliced and grilled red onions, 235 ml (8 fl oz) barbecue sauce and 4 grilled and sliced tomatoes.

company-coming t-bones
Replace the marinade with one made by combining 235 ml (8 fl oz) each of red wine and Worcestershire sauce, 2 tablespoons light brown sugar and 1 tablespoon liquid smoke.

t-bones and wild mushroom medley
Omit the beer marinade. Serve the grilled steaks with a fried mushroom medley using 55g (2 oz) each of butter, chanterelles, champignons and morel mushrooms, or mushrooms of your choice; 1 tablespoon chopped fresh parsley leaves; 120 ml (4 fl oz) brandy; and 1 tablespoon Worcestershire sauce. Cook until tender. Add 120 ml (4 fl oz) double cream and reduce over a high heat to make a thick sauce. Serve with Dijon mustard.

t-bone à la blue
Omit the beer marinade. Serve grilled steaks with a flavoured butter topping made by blending together 225 g (8 oz) crumbled blue cheese, 225 g (8 oz) softened unsalted butter, 25 g (1 oz) breadcrumbs, 2 crushed large garlic cloves and 1 teaspoon cracked black pepper.

t-bones el paso
Replace the marinade with one made by combining 1 sachet taco seasoning, 4 tablespoons olive oil and 1 tablespoon crushed garlic.

variations

grilled marinated sirloin steak

see base recipe page 162

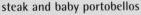

steak and baby portobellos
Replace the marinade with one made by combining 235 ml (8 fl oz) Italian salad dressing,
120 ml (4 fl oz) dry red wine, 1 grated onion, 3 crushed large garlic cloves and 2 tablespoons
chopped fresh oregano. Marinate the steak in this mixture, along with 3 quartered sweet
red peppers and 225 g (8 oz) baby portobello mushrooms. Grill the steak, peppers and
portobellos together.

peppered steak with tarragon
Replace the marinade with a paste made by mixing 3 tablespoons olive oil; 1 tablespoon
green peppercorns, drained and crushed; 3 large garlic cloves, crushed; and 2 tablespoons
chopped fresh tarragon. Proceed as in base recipe.

grilled steaks with martini twist
Replace the marinade with a mixture of 4 tablespoons finely chopped spring onions,
4 tablespoons gin, 1 tablespoon olive oil, 1 teaspoon grated lemon zest, 1 teaspoon freshly
ground tricolored peppercorns and 2 tablespoons sliced pimiento-stuffed green olives.
Proceed as in base recipe.

korean bulgogi
Replace marinade with a mixture of 235 ml (8 fl oz) sesame oil, 475 ml (16 fl oz) soy sauce,
4 crushed large garlic cloves, 1 tablespoon grated fresh ginger and crushed dried chillies to
taste. Proceed as in base recipe.

variations

balsamic rump steaks

see base recipe page 163

rump steaks with shallots

Omit the marinade and balsamic baste. Grill steaks as in the base recipe. Make a sauce for
the sliced grilled steak by sautéing 2 tablespoons unsalted butter, 4 thinly sliced shallots,
2 tablespoons red wine vinegar, 235 ml (8 fl oz) dry red wine and 2 tablespoons chopped
Italian parsley leaves. Cook until reduced to a thick sauce.

grilled rump steaks

Omit the marinade and baste. Simply grill the steaks, seasoning them afterwards with salt
and freshly ground black pepper.

rump steaks with mustard jus

Omit the marinade and baste. Instead make a marinade from 120 ml (4 fl oz) grapefruit juice,
4 tablespoons red wine vinegar and 2 grated shallots. Serve the steak with a sauce made
by simmering together until reduced by half: 1 tablespoon vegetable oil, 4 sliced shallots,
120 ml (4 fl oz) beef consommé, 120 ml (4 fl oz) red wine, 2 tablespoons sweet rice wine,
1 tablespoon Dijon mustard and sugar to taste.

herbed rump steaks

Omit the marinade and baste. Instead drizzle 3 tablespoons olive oil over the cooked steaks
and sprinkle them with 1 tablespoon fresh thyme leaves and 4 thinly sliced large shallots.

fillet steaks with herbed cheese

see base recipe page 164

romanian beef fillet steaks
Omit the cheese mixture. Marinate the tenderloin and 4 large portobello mushrooms in 235 ml (8 fl oz) vegetable oil, 120 ml (4 fl oz) olive oil and 8 crushed large garlic cloves.

beef fillet steaks with mustard tarragon cream sauce
Omit the cheese mixture, garlic rub and parsley garnish. Instead make a sauce for the grilled tenderloin by blending well 4 tablespoons dry white wine, 4 tablespoons sour cream, 1 tablespoon each of Dijon mustard and sugar and 1½ teaspoons chopped fresh tarragon.

grilled southwestern bacon-wrapped beef fillet steaks
Omit the cheese mixture, garlic rub and parsley garnish. Instead wrap each tenderloin in a thick rasher of bacon. Make a rub by combining 1 tablespoon ground cumin, 1 tablespoon chilli powder, 1½ teaspoons paprika, ½ teaspoon cayenne pepper, ¼ teaspoon dried thyme, ¼ teaspoon ground cinnamon and 2 tablespoons vegetable oil. Rub the mixture all over the meat and leave to stand for 30 minutes, before grilling as in the base recipe. Garnish the barbecued steaks with chopped fresh coriander.

grilled beef fillet steaks with herb rub
Omit the cheese mixture, garlic rub and parsley garnish. Instead make a rub by combining 2 teaspoons dried rosemary, 1 teaspoon dried thyme, 1 teaspoon dried tarragon and 2 crushed large garlic cloves. Rub the mixture all over the meat and leave to stand for 30 minutes, before grilling as in the base recipe.

variations

grilled top rump with aïoli

see base recipe page 167

grilled top rump with almond-coriander pesto
Instead of the aïoli, mix the following to make a rub: 1 teaspoon each of sea salt, black pepper, ground cumin, ground coriander and garlic granules; and ¼ teaspoon chilli powder. Rub into the meat and let stand for 30 minutes. Grill as in the base recipe. Serve with a pesto made by mixing 2 tablespoons toasted flaked almonds; 25 g (1 oz) each of fresh coriander and parsley leaves; 1 tablespoon each of chopped and seeded jalapeño and fresh lime juice; 2 crushed garlic cloves; ¼ teaspoon each of salt and black pepper; and 4 tablespoons soured cream.

santa fe top rump
Instead of the aïoli, blend the following to make a marinade: 4 tablespoons vegetable oil, 2 tablespoons each of chopped fresh coriander and parsley, 4 crushed large garlic cloves, 2 teaspoons each of sea salt and ground cumin and 1 teaspoon each of ground coriander, cayenne pepper and black pepper. Marinate steak for 2 hours.

caribbean jerk beef steak
Instead of the aïoli, blend the following marinade: 235 ml (8 fl oz) Italian salad dressing; 2 tablespoons Worcestershire sauce; 1 tablespoon light brown sugar; 1 large jalapeño, seeded and chopped; and 1 teaspoon each of ground allspice and ginger. Marinate the steak for 2 hours.

grilled top rump with nectarines
Omit the aïoli. Marinate the steak for 2 hours in 60 ml (2 fl oz) each of red wine, soy sauce, chicken broth and honey and 1 teaspoon ground ginger. Serve with 4 halved, grilled nectarines.

béarnaise butter

see base recipe page 168

blue cheese, rosemary and balsamic vinegar butter
Instead of making the béarnaise butter, stir the following into the same quantity of
butter: 2 tablespoons each of chopped fresh rosemary leaves and balsamic vinegar,
1 teaspoon Worcestershire sauce, 1 crushed large clove garlic, 55 g (2 oz) crumbled
blue cheese, ½ teaspoon sea salt and ¼ teaspoon freshly ground black pepper.

maître d'hôtel butter (the king of steak butters)
Instead of making the béarnaise butter, stir the following into the same quantity of butter:
4 tablespoons chopped fresh parsley, 4 teaspoons fresh lemon juice, ½ teaspoon sea salt
and ¼ teaspoon freshly ground black pepper.

mild chilli steak butter
Instead of making the béarnaise butter, stir the following into the same quantity of butter:
2 tablespoons finely chopped shallots; 1 tablespoon each of chopped fresh coriander and
finely chopped fresh red chilli pepper, seeded; 1 teaspoon fresh lime juice; 1 teaspoon grated
lime zest, ½ teaspoon sea salt; and ¼ teaspoon freshly ground black pepper.

pesto-walnut butter
Instead of making the béarnaise butter, stir the following into the same quantity of butter:
3 tablespoons each of prepared basil pesto and finely chopped toasted walnuts, ½ teaspoon
sea salt and ¼ teaspoon freshly ground black pepper.

variations

simply grilled sirloin

see base recipe page 169

the perfect sirloin steak

Add a marinade. Combine 2 crushed cloves of garlic; 2 tablespoons each of Worcestershire sauce, soy sauce, balsamic vinegar and olive oil; and 1 tablespoon Dijon mustard. Marinate the steaks for 2 hours, and proceed with the base recipe.

coffee bean and gourmet peppercorn crusted steak

Add a crust: crush 4 tablespoons toasted gourmet peppercorns and 4 tablespoons dark-roasted coffee beans; press into the steaks before grilling. Proceed with the base recipe.

mango sirloin steak

Add a marinade. Heat the following ingredients in a frying pan for 10 minutes: 1 small sliced mango, apple and honeydew melon; 2 tablespoons each Worcestershire sauce and garlic salt; and 1 teaspoon black pepper. Marinate the steaks for 2 hours, and proceed with the base recipe.

steak au poivre rouge

Add a crust: crush 4 tablespoons black peppercorns, 1 tablespoon white peppercorns and 1 teaspoon sea salt; press into the steaks. Proceed with the base recipe. Combine 8 tablespoons softened unsalted butter, 120 ml (4 fl oz) very hearty red wine and 1 tablespoon chopped fresh chives. Top the steaks with this butter when serving.

variations

barbecued beef rib racks

see base recipe page 171

big bill's beef ribs
Replace the rub with one made by mixing 4 tablespoons sea salt; 2 tablespoons each of paprika and coarse ground black pepper; 1½ teaspoons each of garlic granules, onion granules and cayenne pepper; and ½ teaspoon each of ground coriander and turmeric.

beef rib racks with chinese spices
Replace the mop with one made by mixing 120 ml (4 fl oz) hoisin sauce, 4 tablespoons sweet rice wine vinegar, 2 tablespoons clear honey, 2 crushed garlic cloves and 1 tablespoon grated fresh ginger. Replace the rub with one made by mixing 2 tablespoons sea salt, 1 tablespoon each of coarse ground black pepper and Chinese five-spice powder, 2 teaspoons garlic granules and 1 teaspoon ground ginger.

tender smoked beef ribs
Replace the rub with one made by combining 55g (2 oz) sugar; 2 tablespoons each of onion granules, garlic granules, sea salt and Cajun seasoning mix; 1 tablespoon each of black pepper and paprika; 2 teaspoons each of seasoned salt and dried oregano; and ½ teaspoon each of dried sage, grated nutmeg and cayenne pepper.

jack's barbecued sweet beef ribs
Replace mop with 235 ml (8 fl oz) ketchup; 4 tablespoons each of cider vinegar and water; 2 tablespoons each of Worcestershire sauce and brown sugar; 1 tablespoon onion granules; and 1 teaspoon each of dry mustard and paprika; all simmered together for 20 minutes.

variations

devilled chuck steak

see base recipe page 172

barbecued chuck steak
Replace the marinade with one made by mixing 60 ml (2 fl oz) red wine vinegar and
soy sauce; 2 tablespoons each of Worcestershire sauce, brown sugar and vegetable oil;
2 teaspoons each of mustard and garlic salt; and 1 teaspoon freshly ground black pepper.

chuck pepper steak
Replace the marinade with one made by mixing 120 ml (4 fl oz) teriyaki sauce; 60 ml
(2 fl oz) vegetable oil; 2 tablespoons spring onions, thinly sliced; and 1 teaspoon each of
onion granules, garlic granules and celery salt. Top the grilled steaks with 3 green peppers
that have been cut into 1.5 cm (½-in) slices and grilled.

stu's barbecued chuck steak
Replace the marinade with one made by mixing 475 ml (16 fl oz) burgundy, 3 tablespoons
olive oil, 10 to 12 crushed tricolored peppercorns, 1 tablespoon each of sugar and ground
coriander and 1 teaspoon hickory smoked salt.

oriental barbecued chuck steak
Replace the marinade with one made by mixing 235 ml (8 fl oz) pineapple juice; 120 ml
(4 fl oz) soy sauce; 60 ml (2 fl oz) each of sesame oil, grated onions and light brown sugar;
3 crushed large garlic cloves; and 1 tablespoon grated fresh ginger.

argentinian-style rib eye steaks

see base recipe page 174

grilled rib eye steaks with creamed mushrooms

Omit the sauce. Instead marinate the steaks in 60 ml (2 fl oz) soy sauce, 4 crushed large garlic cloves and 1 teaspoon ground cumin. Proceed with the base recipe. Serve with creamed mushrooms made by sautéing, in a large frying pan, 115 g (4 oz) unsalted butter, 455 g (1 lb) sliced fresh mushrooms and 235 ml (8 fl oz) whipping cream; cook until the mushrooms are soft and the cream has reduced by half.

rib doctor rib eye steaks

Omit the sauce. Instead combine seasoned salt, celery salt, garlic salt and onion salt to taste with 8 tablespoons melted unsalted butter. Proceed with the base recipe, using the salted butter mixture as a baste while grilling.

cajun-style rib eye steak

Omit the sauce. Instead make a rub by combining 1 tablespoon paprika, 1 teaspoon each of cayenne pepper and garlic granules and ½ teaspoon each of black and white peppers, onion granules, oregano and thyme. Rub into the steaks and leave to stand for 30 minutes. Proceed with the base recipe.

big billy's cowboy rib eye steaks

Omit the sauce. Instead make a rub by combining 2 tablespoons sea salt and 1 tablespoon each of coarsely ground black pepper, garlic granules, ground thyme and espresso powder. Rub into the steaks and let stand for 30 minutes. Proceed with the base recipe.

variations

grilled chilean skirt steak

see base recipe page 175

spicy grilled skirt steak
Instead of cumin and coriander, flavour the marinade with 1 tablespoon ground coriander.
Replace the relish with one made by combining 1 large red onion, sliced thin; 1 red pepper,
seeded and sliced thin; and 3 tablespoons hot taco sauce or to taste.

grilled garlic skirt steak
Replace the marinade with one made by combining 6 crushed large garlic cloves,
1 teaspoon dry mustard, 1 teaspoon ground cumin, ½ teaspoon powdered bay leaf,
60 ml (2 fl oz) each of Worcestershire sauce and cider vinegar, 1 tablespoon vegetable oil,
1 tablespoon Louisiana hot sauce and 235 ml (8 fl oz) boiling beef broth. Omit the relish.

new mexico grilled skirt steak
Replace the marinade with one made by combining 3 tablespoons of Mexican chilli
powder; 1 tablespoon each of ground cumin, garlic granules and sugar; 2 teaspoons
black pepper; 1 teaspoon ground allspice; 4 tablespoons Worcestershire sauce; and
2 tablespoons vegetable oil. Retain the relish from the base recipe.

amarillo texas marinated skirt steak
Replace the marinade with one made by combining 4 tablespoons each of fresh lemon juice
and olive oil, 1 tablespoon ground cumin, 2 teaspoons chilli powder and 1 teaspoon mild
chilli powder. Retain the relish from the base recipe.

grilled veal chops with rosemary

see base recipe page 177

the baron's grilled veal chops
Replace the marinade with one made by mixing 60 ml (2 fl oz) olive oil with 2 tablespoons each of balsamic vinegar, sea salt, coarse ground black pepper, dried garlic and crushed rosemary. Blend well.

grilled basil veal chops
Replace the rosemary marinade with one made by mixing 3 tablespoons balsamic vinegar, 4 tablespoons each of fresh lemon juice and olive oil, chopped fresh basil leaves, 1 tablespoon each of lemon zest and chopped shallots, 4 crushed garlic cloves and salt and pepper to taste.

grilled lemon-herb veal chops
Replace the rosemary marinade with one made by mixing 3 tablespoons each of extra-virgin olive oil and fresh lemon juice, 3 crushed garlic cloves, 1 tablespoon finely chopped fresh oregano leaves, and 1 teaspoon freshly ground black pepper.

grilled veal chops with roasted garlic paste
Omit the rosemary marinade. Grill the chops as in the base recipe. Make a spice paste by mixing 4 tablespoons roasted garlic, 3 tablespoons softened butter, 2 tablespoons olive oil, 2 tablespoons Dijon mustard and 1 teaspoon mild chilli powder. Rub this paste on to the grilled chops before serving.

variations

barbecued beef ribs

see base recipe page 178

red wine beef ribs
Replace rub with a marinade: mix 120 ml (4 fl oz) dry red wine, 60 ml (2 fl oz) soy sauce,
2 tablespoons vegetable oil, 3 crushed garlic cloves, ½ teaspoon dried thyme and ½ teaspoon
freshly ground black pepper. Marinate the ribs for 2 hours and proceed with base recipe.

grilled korean beef ribs
Replace the rub with a marinade made by mixing 120 ml (4 fl oz) soy sauce, 60 ml (2 fl oz)
dry sherry, 60 ml (2 fl oz) pineapple juice, 2 tablespoons each of sesame oil and sugar and
1 tablespoon grated fresh ginger. Marinate the ribs for 2 hours, and proceed with the base recipe.

grilled texas beef ribs
Replace the rub with a marinade made by mixing 120 ml (4 fl oz) flat lager; 4 tablespoons
each of olive oil, brown sugar and balsamic vinegar; 2 tablespoons each of chilli powder,
seeded and chopped jalapeño, molasses and grated onion; 6 crushed garlic cloves,
1 tablespoon coarse ground black pepper; and 2 teaspoons sea salt. Marinate the ribs
for 2 hours, and proceed with the base recipe.

spicy kansas city grilled beef ribs
Replace the rub with a Kansas City rub made with a mixture of 4 tablespoons light brown
sugar; 2 tablespoons each of garlic salt and seasoned salt; 1 tablespoon chilli powder;
1 teaspoon each of ground allspice, black pepper, ground cumin and ground ginger;
½ teaspoon mild chilli powder; and ½ teaspoon ground cinnamon.

variations

grilled sirloin roast

see base recipe page 179

tasty tequila sirloin roast
Replace the rub with a marinade made by mixing 60 ml (2 fl oz) tequila; 2 tablespoons each of sesame oil, Dijon mustard and balsamic vinegar; 2 crushed large garlic cloves; and 2 teaspoons each of sea salt and freshly ground black pepper. Marinate for 2 hours, and proceed with the base recipe.

spicy grilled beef sirloin roast
Substitute the following for the rub ingredients: 2 tablespoons onion granules, 2 heaped tablespoons light brown sugar, 1 tablespoon paprika, 1 tablespoon chilli powder, 1 teaspoon cayenne pepper, sea salt to taste and ½ teaspoon each of ground cumin and cinnamon.

teriyaki marinated sirloin
Replace the rub with a marinade made by mixing 120 ml (4 fl oz) each of burgundy wine and teriyaki sauce, 60 ml (2 fl oz) each of vegetable oil and soy sauce, 5 tablespoons red wine vinegar, 1 tablespoon paprika, 1 tablespoon crushed dried parsley and 3 crushed large garlic cloves. Marinate for 2 hours, and proceed with the base recipe.

santa maria–style grilled sirloin
Replace the rub with one made by mixing 6 tablespoons sea salt, 4 tablespoons garlic granules, 2 tablespoons paprika, 1 tablespoon each of coarse ground black pepper and white pepper, 2 teaspoons cayenne pepper and 1 teaspoon onion granules. While grilling, baste with a mixture of 120 ml (4 fl oz) each of red wine vinegar and garlic-infused vegetable oil.

vegetarian bites

Fresh vegetables with a seared crusty edge are one
of the most appetising elements of any barbecue.
Try your hand at some of our simple veggie grills, or
make them the centrepiece of your meal by putting
together a colourful assorted platter.

grilled lollipop onions

see variations page 219

Grilled onions lose their acrid flavour, becoming soft and smoky with a sweet edge.

4 sweet or mild onions, peeled and cut into
    1.5 cm- (¹/₂ in-) thick slices
12 to 16 grilling skewers

Sea salt and freshly ground black pepper to
    taste
2 tbsp vegetable oil

Preheat the barbecue to medium. Carefully insert a skewer through each of the onion slices. Season both sides of the onions with salt and pepper; brush with vegetable oil. Be careful: too much oil will cause flare-ups on the barbecue.

Barbecue the onions, covered, for about 5 minutes. Turn over; brush with vegetable oil; and grill for 5 to 7 more minutes or until tender.

Serves 8

roasted garlic grilled tomatoes

see variations page 220

The appetising scents of an Italian kitchen will draw your guests to the barbecue when you prepare these simple yet sophisticated tomatoes.

6 ripe tomatoes
Coarse salt and freshly ground black pepper
3 tbsp extra-virgin olive oil
2 tbsp butter, melted

8 cloves roasted garlic
25 to 55 g (1 to 2 oz) Parmesan cheese
1 tsp dried thyme

Cut the tomatoes in half crossways. Season with salt and pepper and set aside. Heat the oil and butter in a small frying pan. Add the roasted garlic and cook for 1 to 2 minutes until well blended and incorporated. Pour the garlic mixture into a heatproof bowl.

Preheat the barbecue to high. If using a gas grill, place wood chips, if desired, in the smoker box and preheat until you see smoke. If using a charcoal grill, toss the wood chips, if desired, on the coals. Place the tomatoes cut-side down on the hot barbecue and grill until nicely browned, 3 to 5 minutes, rotating them 45 degrees after 2 minutes to create an attractive crosshatch of grill marks. Turn the tomatoes with tongs, spoon the fried garlic over the tomatoes and continue grilling for 3 to 5 minutes, until the bottoms are nicely browned.

Transfer the tomatoes to a platter. Grate the Parmesan over the tomatoes and sprinkle them with the thyme. Serve at once.

Serves 3

spicy grilled aubergine

see variations page 221

Fresh herbs and a squeeze of lemon make a vibrant partnership with the smoky taste of grilled aubergine.

1 large aubergine, cut into 1.5 cm- (½ in-) thick slices
1 to 2 tsp salt, to remove water from aubergine
2 tbsp olive oil
2 tsp red wine vinegar
2 tsp fresh lemon juice
1 tsp pressed garlic

1 tsp crushed dried chillies
1 tsp herb seasoning mix
2 tbsp olive oil, to brush aubergine for barbecuing
1 tbsp chopped fresh parsley
1 tbsp chopped fresh mint

Put the aubergine slices in a colander in a single layer and sprinkle with salt. Leave to drain for 20 minutes, then turn, sprinkle the other side with salt and leave to drain for 20 minutes more. While the aubergine drains, whisk together the olive oil, wine vinegar, lemon juice, garlic, crushed chillies and herb seasoning. Set the spicy sauce aside.

Preheat a barbecue to medium. Press each aubergine slice between 2 pieces of kitchen paper to dry them. Brush both sides with olive oil. Place the aubergine on the grill and cook for 4 to 5 minutes per side, rotating after a few minutes on each side if you want to get grill marks. Watch the aubergine slices carefully because they go from gently browned to charred quickly. When the aubergine is cooked, remove from the grill and place in a large bowl. Stir in the spicy sauce to coat. Leave to cool slightly, then sprinkle the parsley and mint over the aubergine and serve warm or at room temperature.

Serves 4

grilled sweet potatoes

see variations page 222

Parboiling before barbecuing cuts down the actual cooking time, making this a quick and simple vegetable dish.

4 to 6 medium sweet potatoes, scrubbed
60 ml (2 fl oz) vegetable oil
Sea salt and freshly ground pepper to taste

Parboil the sweet potatoes for 10 minutes, then allow them to cool. Cut each one into 6 or 8 slices or wedges. Brush the potatoes all over with oil. Preheat the barbecue, then cook the sweet potatoes over medium heat for 5 to 7 minutes on each side, until crisp and lightly browned. Season with salt and pepper.

Serves 4–6

grilled herbed potatoes

see variations page 223

Turn the potatoes through 90 degrees halfway through cooking to obtain attractive chargrilled scorch marks on all the slices.

4 medium potatoes, brushed and washed
2 tbsp olive oil
6 thinly sliced spring onions
4 tbsp olive oil
3 tbsp grated Parmesan cheese

3 tbsp chopped fresh parsley
2 tbsp chopped fresh oregano
3 cloves garlic, pressed
Salt and pepper to taste

Cook the potatoes in a large pan of boiling salted water until tender. Drain and leave to cool. Cut the potatoes into wedges or slices and place in a large bowl. Add 2 tablespoons of olive oil and toss to mix.

Grill the potatoes on a barbecue preheated to medium for 5 minutes, turning occasionally. Transfer to a bowl. Add the remaining oil, the Parmesan, herbs and garlic, and toss to mix. Season with salt and pepper to taste.

Serves 4

asparagus with black pepper

see variations page 224

A vegetable as elegant as asparagus suits simple preparations like this one.

455 g (1 lb) asparagus
Sea salt and freshly ground black pepper
to taste

Snap or cut off any woody ends from the asparagus spears; soak the spears in cold water for 30 minutes. Cook the asparagus diagonally on a barbecue preheated to medium until the ends begin to soften. Turn the spears across the grill to obtain grill marks, being careful to keep them at a diagonal angle so they don't fall through.

Be careful not to overcook the spears or to let them get too brown. Season with sea salt and freshly ground black pepper to taste.

Serves 4

grilled patty pan squash

see variations page 225

These tiny squash are available in specialist greengrocers; thick slices of courgette would work equally well.

60 ml (2 fl oz) extra-virgin olive oil
2 tsp grated onion
1 tsp dried marjoram
1 large clove garlic, pressed

12 small patty pan squash
Grated cheddar or Parmesan to serve (optional)

Combine the olive oil and all of the flavourings, blend well and set aside.

Cut the squash lengthways and remove the seeds. Wash thoroughly in cold water and pat dry. Preheat a grill to medium. Brush the squash on one side with the olive oil mixture and place face down on the grill.

Cover and cook for 6 to 10 minutes, turning halfway through cooking. Brush the squash with more of the olive oil mixture, turn over and cover again. Cook until the squash is golden brown on both sides.

Serve hot, sprinkled with grated cheddar or Parmesan, if you like.

Serves 6

grilled vegetable platter with balsamic maple dressing

see variations page 226

The bright colours of the vegetables piled high on this platter look really spectacular.

455 g (1 lb) thick asparagus spears
2 courgettes
255 g (8 oz) carrots, peeled
1 red pepper
1 yellow pepper
1 large red onion, peeled
2 tbsp vegetable oil

1 tbsp fresh thyme
Sea salt and freshly ground black pepper to
  taste
120 ml (4 fl oz) balsamic vinegar
60 ml (2 fl oz) maple syrup

Trim the woody ends from the asparagus spears. Cut the courgettes and carrots lengthways into thirds. Seed and core the red and yellow peppers; cut each into eighths. Cut the onion into 8 wedges, leaving the end intact. Place the vegetables in a bowl. Toss the vegetables with the oil, thyme, salt and pepper. Place the vegetables on a barbecue which has been preheated to medium. Close the lid and cook for 3 minutes. Remove the asparagus and keep warm. Rotate the remaining vegetables 90 degrees to make grill marks. Cover the barbecue again. Continue cooking, rotating every 3 minutes, until just tender. Remove from the heat.

Meanwhile, in a small saucepan, bring the vinegar and maple syrup to the boil and boil for about 2 minutes, until thickened. Brush ¼ of the glaze over vegetables; turn over and brush again. Transfer to a serving platter and brush them with the remaining glaze.

Serves 6

vegetable kebabs

see variations page 227

Prepare these kebabs using whatever vegetables are in season or to hand from the suggestions below.

1 aubergine, cut into cubes
1 red pepper, cut into strips
2 red onions, cut into wedges
16 medium-sized button mushrooms
8 cherry tomatoes
1 medium cucumber, cut into 8 slices
1 stalk celery cut into 2.5 cm (1 in) pieces
Water-soaked skewers

120 ml (4 fl oz) fresh lemon juice
Grated zest of 2 lemons
1 tbsp olive oil
2 pressed large cloves garlic
1 tbsp chopped fresh thyme
8 tbsp chopped fresh herbs
Salt and freshly ground black pepper to taste

Thread the vegetables onto skewers, alternating the colours to make them look more attractive, and place on a large dish. Sprinkle with the lemon juice and zest, oil, garlic and thyme. Marinate for 1 hour, turning occasionally. Preheat the barbecue to medium.

Before grilling, roll the skewers in your favourite combination of fresh herbs. Place the skewers directly on the grill, about 7.5 to 10 cm (3 to 4 in) from the heat source. Cover and barbecue for 15 to 20 minutes or until tender and brown, turning frequently.

Serves 4–6

creole-style stuffed mushrooms

see variations page 228

The type of mushrooms you choose will determine how much filling you will need, so adjust the recipes as needed

455 g (1 lb) button mushrooms
1 tsp olive oil
4 tbsp grated onion
4 tbsp finely chopped red pepper
280 g (10 oz) frozen spinach, thawed and drained

$2^1/_2$ slices whole wheat bread, torn into breadcrumbs
1 tsp Creole or Cajun seasoning mix
$^1/_4$ tsp ground turmeric
55 g (2 oz) grated cheddar cheese

Preheat the barbecue smoker to 120°C (250°F). Lightly coat a shallow baking tin or mini-muffin tins with oil. Remove the mushroom stems from the caps. Finely chop the stems. Reserve the caps and set aside.

Heat the olive oil in a large frying pan over high heat. Sauté the chopped mushroom stems, onion, pepper and spinach for about 5 minutes or until tender. Remove the frying pan from the heat and stir in the breadcrumbs and seasonings until well combined.

Stuff each mushroom cap with 2 tablespoons of the filling mixture. Place the mushrooms, stuffed sides up, on the baking tin. Place in the barbecue or smoker, cover and cook for about 45 minutes to 1 hour. A few minutes before the end of cooking, remove from the grill and sprinkle the cheese on the top. Place back in the smoker to finish cooking. Serve warm.

Serves 2–3

crunchy nut burgers

see variations page 229

You could use any crunchy, not-too-sweet breakfast cereal or muesli for this veggie burger recipe.

2 eggs, well beaten
120 ml (4 fl oz) vegetable juice
1 packet dry onion soup mix
5 tablespoons tomato ketchup
225 g (8 oz) crunchy nut cereal

Sea salt and freshly ground black pepper
Oil for brushing
Wholemeal rolls, toasted
Lettuce, sliced onions and sliced tomatoes
   to garnish

In a large bowl, whisk together the eggs, vegetable juice, onion soup mix and ketchup. Work in the cereal. Cover and refrigerate for 4 or 5 hours or overnight. Form into 8 patties.

Prepare a medium-hot barbecue. Brush the burgers with a little oil and grill over medium heat, covered, for about 4 to 5 minutes on each side. Brush the top of the burgers with a little more oil before turning. Allow them to brown on each side. Using a grill basket will make turning these much easier. Serve in the wholemeal rolls and garnish with lettuce, sliced onions and sliced tomatoes.

Makes 8

variations

grilled lollipop onions

see base recipe page 199

grilled red onions
Replace the sweet onions with halved medium red onions. Omit the vegetable oil, salt and pepper. Instead, marinate the onions for 2 hours in a mixture made from 2 tablespoons each of Worcestershire sauce, balsamic vinegar, soy sauce and olive oil; with sea salt and freshly ground black pepper to taste. Drain before grilling.

zesty grilled baby onions
Replace the sweet onions with 24 baby onions, parboiled for 5 minutes. Thread them onto 4 bamboo skewers. Omit the vegetable oil, salt and pepper. Instead, brush them with a mixture made from 120 ml (4 fl oz) each of Italian salad dressing and sweet onion salad dressing, 8 tablespoons melted unsalted butter and sea salt and coarse ground black pepper to taste. Baste.

mexican grilled onions
Prepare the base recipe, seasoning the onions before grilling with taco seasoning to taste.

beer and cayenne grilled onions
Omit vegetable oil, salt and pepper. Marinate the sliced onions for 2 hours in a mixture of 350 ml (12 fl oz) beer; 115 g (4 oz) melted unsalted butter; 2 tablespoons olive oil; and sea salt, freshly ground black pepper and cayenne pepper to taste. Drain, reserving the marinade. Skewer and grill as in the base recipe, using the marinade to baste regularly.

variations

roasted garlic grilled tomatoes

see base recipe page 200

grilled green tomatoes
Omit the roasted garlic, oil and butter. Replace the red tomatoes with 4 large green tomatoes, sliced 1.5 cm- (½ in-) thick. Make a topping or dip by combining 60 ml (2 fl oz) each of sour cream, mayonnaise and sweet chilli sauce.

grilled tomato melts
Omit the roasted garlic, oil, butter, Parmesan and thyme. Five minutes before the end of grilling, top the tomatoes with 175 g (6 oz) grated cheddar cheese, 55 g (2 oz) chopped red pepper, and 25 g (1 oz) toasted sliced almonds.

herb-grilled tomatoes
Omit the roasted garlic, oil, butter, Parmesan and thyme. Replace the fried garlic topping with a mixture of 120 ml (4 fl oz) sour cream or plain yogurt and 3 tablespoons each of chopped fresh basil, fine dry breadcrumbs and finely grated Parmesan cheese. Garnish with 4 to 5 fresh basil sprigs.

spicy grilled tomatoes
Omit everything except the tomatoes. Replace the fried garlic topping with a mixture of 1 finely chopped fresh red chilli, seeded and chopped; 235 ml (8 fl oz) plain yogurt; and 1 teaspoon each of onion granules, sugar and curry powder. Use as a topping for the grilled tomatoes.

variations

spicy grilled aubergine

see base recipe page 203

honey-garlic grilled aubergine
Omit the olive oil for brushing onto the aubergine. Replace the herbs and the spicy sauce with a marinade made by mixing 2 tablespoons clear honey, 2 tablespoons olive oil, 2 pressed large cloves garlic, 1 tablespoon smoked paprika, 2 teaspoons balsamic vinegar and salt and pepper to taste. Marinate for 2 hours. Drain and cook, basting with the reserved marinade.

herb and garlic grilled aubergine
Omit the olive oil for brushing onto the aubergine. Replace the herbs and the spicy sauce with a marinade made by mixing 150 ml (5 fl oz) extra-virgin olive oil, 4 pressed large cloves garlic, 8 tablespoons each of chopped fresh basil and flat-leaf parsley, salt to taste and $\frac{1}{8}$ teaspoon freshly ground black pepper. Leave to marinate for 2 hours. Drain and cook, basting with the reserved marinade.

grilled aubergine
Omit the olive oil for brushing onto the aubergine. Replace the herbs and the spicy sauce with a marinade made by mixing 3 tablespoons olive oil; 2 tablespoons balsamic vinegar; 2 cloves garlic, very finely chopped; 1 pinch each of dried thyme, basil, dill and oregano; and salt and pepper to taste. Marinate for 2 hours. Drain and cook, basting with the reserved marinade.

garlic-butter grilled aubergine
Omit the olive oil for brushing onto the aubergine. Replace the herbs and spicy sauce with a baste: combine 115 g (4 oz) butter at room temperature and 4 pressed cloves garlic.

variations

grilled sweet potatoes

see base recipe page 204

grilled sweet potato sticks
Place the potato pieces on 4 water-soaked bamboo skewers. Instead of the oil, brush the potatoes with 70 g (2½ oz) melted butter, 2 tablespoons soy sauce and 1 tablespoon toasted sesame seeds. Grill like kebabs, turning regularly.

grilled candied sweet potatoes
Omit the vegetable oil. Stir together 4 tablespoons light brown sugar and 2 tablespoons lemon juice. Grill the potatoes as in the base recipe, brushing regularly with the sugar and lemon mixture so that they form a caramelised crust.

jamaican grilled sweet potatoes
Omit the vegetable oil. Stir together 4 tablespoons light brown sugar, 2 tablespoons softened butter, 1 teaspoon ground ginger, ½ teaspoon ground allspice, 1 tablespoon dark rum and 1 tablespoon chopped fresh coriander. Grill the potatoes as in the base recipe, brushing regularly with this mixture while cooking.

cinnamon-grilled sweet potatoes
Omit the vegetable oil. Stir together 70 g (2½ oz) melted butter, 2 tablespoons granulated sugar and 1 teaspoon cinnamon sugar. Grill the potatoes as in the base recipe, brushing regularly with this mixture while cooking.

grilled herbed potatoes

see base recipe page 207

grilled potatoes tuscan-style
Replace the onions, cheese, parsley and oregano with 5 chopped fresh sage leaves and 2 teaspoons chopped fresh rosemary. Proceed with the base recipe.

grilled potatoes with roasted garlic
Replace the 4 tablespoons olive oil, onions, cheese, parsley, oregano and garlic with 2 heads smoked or roasted garlic, blended to a paste with 4 tablespoons extra-virgin olive oil. Garnish the cooked potatoes with 2 tablespoons chopped fresh parsley. Proceed with the base recipe.

honey-grilled potatoes
Replace the onions, cheese, parsley, oregano and garlic with 2 tablespoons finely chopped onions, 2 tablespoons clover honey, and 1 teaspoon dry mustard. Proceed with the base recipe.

simple grilled potatoes
Replace the onions, cheese, garlic, oregano and parsley with 2 teaspoons salt. Replace the 4 tablespoons olive oil with 55 g (2 oz) melted butter. Proceed with the base recipe.

scandinavian herbed potatoes
Omit the onions, cheese, oil, herbs and garlic. Replace them with 3 tablespoons chopped fresh dill and 8 crushed juniper berries. Proceed with the base recipe.

variations

asparagus with black pepper

see base recipe page 208

asparagus with honey-garlic sauce
Prepare the base recipe. Serve the grilled asparagus with a sauce made by stirring together 4 tablespoons Dijon mustard, 4 tablespoons dark beer, 3 tablespoons clear honey, 1 teaspoon pressed garlic and ¼ teaspoon dried thyme.

grilled sesame asparagus
Prepare the base recipe. Serve the grilled asparagus with a sauce made by stirring together 2 tablespoons soy sauce, 2 tablespoons sweet rice wine vinegar, 1 tablespoon toasted sesame oil, 1 tablespoon sesame seeds and 1 finely chopped fresh mild chilli.

grilled asparagus with red onion and orange
Prepare the base recipe, basting the asparagus while grilling with a mixture of 4 tablespoons each of chopped celery, and chopped red onion, 1 tablespoon grated carrot, 1 tablespoon peeled and grated fresh ginger, 1 teaspoon grated orange zest, 5 tablespoons unsweetened apple juice, 2 tablespoons rice wine vinegar and 1 tablespoon clear honey. Drizzle any excess basting mixture over the finished asparagus.

grilled asparagus with red pepper sauce
Prepare the base recipe. Serve the grilled asparagus with a sauce made by stirring together 2 roasted red peppers, finely chopped; 2 cloves garlic, pressed; 3 tablespoons red wine vinegar; 2 tablespoons olive oil; and 4 tablespoons torn fresh basil leaves.

grilled patty pan squash

see base recipe page 211

grilled squash
Omit the marjoram, garlic and onion. Grill the squash as in the base recipe, basting regularly with 2 tablespoons melted butter in place of the oil.

oregano grilled squash
Omit the marjoram, garlic and onion. Grill the squash as in the base recipe. Garnish the cooked squash with 1 tablespoon chopped fresh oregano.

onion and rosemary grilled squash
Replace the marjoram and onion with 2 red onions, cut into 2 cm- (¾ in-) thick slices; ½ teaspoon crushed dried chillies; and ½ teaspoon dried rosemary.

grilled squash parmesan
Replace the marjoram, garlic and onion with 2 diced tomatoes and ½ teaspoon dried oregano. Before the last minute on the grill, sprinkle the squash with grated Parmesan.

summertime grilled squash
Prepare the base recipe, pouring over the grilled squash a topping made by stirring 3 tablepoons chopped fresh mint into 120 ml (4 fl oz) plain yogurt.

grilled vegetable platter with balsamic maple dressing

see base recipe page 212

tuscan grilled summer vegetables
Add to the platter 3 sliced ripe tomatoes and 28 g (1 oz) chopped fresh basil. Replace the dressing with a marinade made by mixing together 60 ml (2 fl oz) each of red wine and olive oil; 1 tablespoon each of chopped fresh sage and rosemary; 1 tablespoon crushed black peppercorns; 1 tablespoon grated orange zest; and 2 pressed cloves garlic. Marinate the vegetables for 30 minutes. Drain, then grill as in the base recipe.

grilled vegetables with basil aïoli
Prepare the platter as in the base recipe. Replace the dressing with a basil aïoli made by whisking together 4 tablespoons torn basil leaves, 2 pressed large cloves garlic, 1 egg yolk, 2 teaspoons fresh lemon juice and 120 ml (4 fl oz) olive oil. The oil must be added gradually in a thin stream, not all at once. Put the aïoli in a bowl to serve with the vegetables.

grilled vegetable platter with fresh basil vinaigrette
Prepare the platter as in the base recipe. Replace the dressing with a vinaigrette made by whisking together 235 ml (8 fl oz) extra-virgin olive oil, 60 ml (2 fl oz) fresh lemon juice, 4 tablespoons chopped fresh basil, 2 pressed cloves garlic and 1 tablespoon Dijon mustard.

mediterranean grilled vegetables
Marinate the vegetables for 30 minutes in a mixture of 235 ml (8 fl oz) olive oil and 5 tablespoons Italian seasoning, before proceeding with the base recipe.

variations

vegetable kebabs

see base recipe page 215

fruit and vegetable kebabs
Replace the lemon juice, zest, olive oil, garlic and herbs with 3 tablespoons olive oil, 2 tablespoons cider vinegar and 2 tablespoons orange juice. Alternate the vegetables on the skewers with 175 g (6 oz) dried apricots and 2 thickly sliced bananas.

vegetable kebabs with cherry tomatoes
Double the quantity of cherry tomatoes on the kebabs. Drizzle with olive oil after grilling.

teriyaki tofu and fruit kebabs
Omit the marinade. Replace the vegetables with 340 g (12 oz) firm tofu, drained and cut into 32 cubes, and 225 g (8 oz) pineapple chunks. Stir the following ingredients together to use as a marinade: 120 ml (4 fl oz) orange juice, 2 tablespoons soy sauce, 2 tablespoons light brown sugar, 2 pressed cloves garlic and 1 tablespoon peeled and grated fresh ginger. Grill as in the base recipe.

teriyaki kebabs
Add to the kebabs 2 corn cobs, cut into 5 cm (2 in) chunks. Grill as in the base recipe, basting regularly with 235 ml (8 fl oz) teriyaki sauce.

vegetable kebabs with sour cream dressing
Prepare the base recipe. Alongside the kebabs, serve a bowl of dressing made by stirring 1 pressed clove garlic and 1 tablespoon chopped fresh chives into 120 ml (4 fl oz) sour cream.

creole-style stuffed mushrooms

see base recipe page 216

grilled stuffed portobello mushrooms
Replace the red pepper, breadcrumbs, Cajun seasoning, turmeric and cheese with 115 g (4 oz) chopped fresh tomatoes; 4 tablespoons each sun-dried tomatoes and black olives; and 2 pressed cloves garlic. Retain the spinach and onion. Use to stuff portobello caps.

mushrooms napoleon
Replace the onions, spinach, red pepper, Cajun seasoning, turmeric and cheese with 1 large tomato, seeded and chopped; 3 tablespoons each chopped flat-leaf parsley and extra-virgin olive oil; 1 tablespoon each chopped fresh basil and red wine vinegar; 9 slices bread, torn into crumbs; and 55 g (2 oz) shaved Parmesan cheese. Garnish the cooked mushrooms with fresh basil sprigs.

cajun-style portobello mushrooms
Omit the stuffing and leave the mushroom stems intact. Omit the cheese. Grill the mushrooms as in the base recipe and season them afterward with 1 teaspoon Cajun seasoning. Drizzle over them a dressing made by combining 2 tablespoons Worcestershire sauce, 2 tablespoons balsamic vinegar, and 1 tablespoon olive oil.

paul's grilled mushrooms
Omit the stuffing, seasoning, and cheese. Leave the mushroom stems intact. Grill the mushrooms as in the base recipe and drizzle 120 ml (4 fl oz) Italian salad dressing over them after grilling.

crunchy nut burgers

see base recipe page 218

veggie burgers
Replace the eggs, juice, soup mix, ketchup and crunchy nut cereal with a mixture of a 400 g (14 oz) can kidney beans, rinsed and drained; 55 g (2 oz) each of rolled oats, chopped fresh mushrooms, chopped onion and chopped red pepper; 1 grated carrot; and 2 pressed cloves garlic. Proceed with the base recipe.

zesty white bean burgers
Replace 1 of the eggs, the juice, soup mix, ketchup and crunchy nut cereal with a 400 g (14 oz) can cannellini beans, mashed with a fork; a 140 g (5 oz) jar chopped green chillies; 2 spring onions, thinly sliced; 90 g (3½ oz) dry breadcrumbs; and 4 tablespoons polenta. Proceed with the base recipe.

portobello mushroom sandwich
Replace the juice, soup mix, ketchup and crunchy nut cereal with 125 g (4½ oz) chopped portobello mushroom caps and 2 tablespoons olive oil. There is no need to refrigerate this mixture. Form into patties and grill as in the base recipe.

pepper sandwich
Omit the burger mixture. Make a different filling for the rolls by grilling 2 red and 1 yellow peppers, seeded and sliced; and 1 large red onion, sliced 1.5 cm (½ in) thick. Lay the grilled vegetables on the open rolls and drizzle Italian salad dressing over them. Top with the remaining roll halves.

salads and sides

Cool crunchy salads and tasty side dishes complete your barbecue feast. The dishes here are suited to being served alongside any of the main dishes in the earlier chapters. You could try Spanish coleslaw for a light accompaniment to fish or steak or make a vegetarian barbecue more substantial with a potato salad or bean casserole.

potato salad with cucumber and dill

see variations page 248

The tangy combination of cucumber and dill adds a Scandinavian note to this otherwise classic potato salad.

1.35 kg (3 lbs) red-skinned potatoes, unpeeled
28 g (1 oz) chopped spring onions, green and white parts
1 cucumber, sliced lengthways, and then sliced across

28 g (1 oz) chopped fresh dill
150 ml (5 fl oz) olive oil
4 tbsp white wine vinegar
1 tbsp Dijon mustard
Sea salt and freshly ground black pepper

Roughly chop the unpeeled potatoes and then boil them in a large pan of salted water until tender. Drain and cool. In a large bowl, combine the potatoes, spring onions, cucumber slices and dill.

In a separate small bowl, mix together the olive oil, vinegar and mustard. Pour this dressing over the potato mixture. Season with salt and pepper. Toss until the salad is thoroughly mixed. Store in the refrigerator in an airtight container until needed.

Serves 6

picnic-style potato salad

see variations page 249

Remove this salad from the refrigerator an hour or two before serving to allow the flavours to return to life.

1.35 kg (3 lbs) red-skinned potatoes
115 g (4 oz) diced celery
55 g (2 oz) diced, seeded cucumber
40 g (1½ oz) sliced spring onions
285 ml (10 fl oz) low-fat mayonnaise
1 tbsp prepared yellow mustard

1 tbsp granulated sugar
1 tbsp fresh lemon juice
55 g (2 oz) grated mature cheddar cheese
3 hard-boiled eggs, chopped
Sea salt and cracked black pepper, to taste

Cut small red potatoes in half, large ones into quarters. Place in a large saucepan and cover with water. Bring to the boil and cook for about 14 to 20 minutes, until tender. Drain and chill. Toss the potatoes in a large bowl with the celery, diced cucumber and onions. Blend the mayonnaise, mustard, sugar, lemon juice, cheese, eggs, salt and pepper. Pour over the potato mixture and toss gently. Cover and chill for at least 4 hours or overnight to blend the flavours.

Serves 6

barbecued corn on the cob

see variations page 250

Here's the classic barbecue vegetable.

8 corn cobs
40 g (1½ oz) butter
1 tsp chilli powder

1 tsp onion salt
Freshly ground black pepper, to taste

Pull the husks carefully from the corn so that each husk remains attached to the bottom of the ear. Remove any silk from the corn.

Melt the butter in a small saucepan, add the seasonings and stir. Brush this butter mixture on to each corn cob. Pull the corn husk up to cover the corn and wrap each piece in a sheet of heavy-duty foil.

Preheat the barbecue, then grill the corn directly over a medium-hot charcoal fire. Cook for 30 to 40 minutes, turning every few minutes. Carefully remove the foil and husk before serving.

Makes 8

spanish coleslaw

see variations page 251

This is sharper and lighter than the classic coleslaw because it replaces the typical mayonnaise dressing with a tangy oil and vinegar dressing.

600 g (1 lb 5 oz) green cabbage, shredded
115 g (4 oz) red cabbage, shredded
55 g (2 oz) diced red pepper or pimiento
4 tbsp diced green pepper
5 tbsp white wine vinegar
4 tbsp vegetable oil

3 tbsp finely chopped onion
2 tbsp granulated sugar
1 tsp celery salt
1 tsp dry mustard
Sea salt and freshly ground black pepper

In a large bowl, combine the cabbages and red and green pepper. Place the remaining ingredients in a small jar with a tight-fitting lid. Screw on the lid and shake well to combine. Pour the dressing over the cabbage mixture just before serving and toss to coat. Serve with a slotted spoon.

Serves 6

garlic bread

see variations page 252

Another way to cook garlic bread is to barbecue the unbuttered and unsliced bread for about 2 minutes, brush with the butter mixture, grill for 1 to 2 minutes more and serve it cut into 5 cm (2 in) slices.

1 loaf ciabatta or French bread
115 g (4 oz) soft butter
2 crushed large cloves garlic
1 tsp dried parsley

$\frac{1}{4}$ tsp dried oregano
$\frac{1}{4}$ tsp dried dill
Freshly grated Parmesan cheese, to taste
Dried parsley, for sprinkling

Cut the bread into 2.5 cm (1 in) slices but do not cut all the way through. Blend the butter, garlic, parsley, oregano and dill. Spread this mixture on both sides of the bread slices. Put the loaf back together on a large piece of kitchen foil. Shape the foil around the loaf of bread. Twist the ends of the foil to seal, but leave the top open. Sprinkle the top liberally with cheese and additional dried parsley. Preheat the barbecue, place the bread on the grill away from the heat and cook for 30 minutes to 1 hour, until lightly toasted. The timing depends on the temperature.

Serves 4

green beans au gratin

see variations page 253

This tasty oven-cooked dish is ideal to serve al fresco in warmer weather. It goes well with both grilled meat and fish.

455 g (1 lb) green beans (fresh or frozen)
2 tbsp butter
3 tbsp plain flour
235 ml (8 fl oz) milk
115 g (4 oz) mature cheddar cheese, grated
1 tbsp prepared mustard

$1/8$ tsp freshly ground black pepper
$1/2$ tsp salt
4 tbsp breadcrumbs tossed with 1 tbsp
    melted butter

Top and tail the beans and boil them in salted water until tender. Drain the beans and reserve 120 ml (4 fl oz) of the cooking liquid.

Melt the butter in a saucepan and whisk in the flour. Add the milk slowly and cook over a low heat until thickened, stirring constantly. Add the cheese, mustard and reserved cooking liquid to the pan. Stir constantly until the cheese melts. Add the salt and pepper. Place alternating layers of green beans and sauce in a greased baking dish, then top with the buttered breadcrumbs. Bake at 180°C (350°F / Gas mark 4) for 30 minutes and serve hot.

Serves 4

baked beans

see variations page 254

A classic American barbecue dish that makes a warming addition to any meal.

455 g (1 lb) streaky bacon, chopped
1 onion, peeled and chopped
1 green pepper, chopped
Two 425 g (15 oz) tins baked beans with pork
   sausages

235 ml (8 fl oz) barbecue sauce
225 g (8 oz) light brown sugar

In a large frying pan, fry the bacon until cooked and crisp. Drain on kitchen paper. Add the onion and green pepper to the reserved fat in the frying pan and cook until soft. Drain to remove excess grease. Empty the beans into a casserole dish and add the bacon, onions, pepper, barbecue sauce and sugar. Stir to combine. Bake at 180°C (350°F / Gas mark 4) for 45 minutes. Serve hot or, if preferred, at room temperature.

Serves 4

caribbean pinto beans

see variations page 255

Mottled pink pinto beans cook to a creamy texture that makes this dish perfect comfort food. It's an ideal way of using up leftover barbecued meat, too.

2 tbsp olive oil
2 Spanish onions, chopped
1 red pepper, chopped
2 cloves garlic, crushed
455 g (1 lb) dried pinto beans, rinsed and
    cleaned
120 ml (4 fl oz) water

2 tsp salt
2 tsp freshly ground black pepper
1 tsp ground allspice
340 g (12 oz) barbecued pork
235 ml (8 fl oz) barbecue sauce

Warm the oil in a frying pan over a medium-high heat and add the onion, pepper and garlic. Sauté for about 5 minutes, until just soft.

Combine the beans, onion, pepper, garlic and water in a heavy-based pan and bring to the boil. Reduce heat to a steady simmer, stirring occasionally and making sure that the mixture doesn't burn. Cook for about 30 to 45 minutes, until soft and heated through. Add the salt, pepper and ground allspice. Stir in the meat and barbecue sauce. Simmer for about 10 minutes more until the beans are soft and milky.

Serves 6

garlic and dill grilled potatoes

see variations page 256

Plain baked potatoes are standard, clichéd barbecue fare – this recipe takes the dish to another level.

6 large potatoes, peeled and sliced
1 onion, halved and sliced
3 cloves garlic, crushed
1 tbsp chopped fresh dill
40 g (1½ oz) unsalted butter

115 g (4 oz) Cheddar cheese, grated
Sea salt and freshly ground black pepper,
    to taste

Preheat the barbecue. Place the potatoes, topped with the onion, garlic, dill and butter, on a large sheet of heavy-duty foil. Seal the potatoes in the foil and place on the grill. Cook for 20 minutes over a high heat. Turn the foil parcel over once during the cooking process.

In the last 5 minutes of cooking, open the foil and sprinkle the potatoes with Cheddar. Reseal the foil parcels and cook for an additional 5 to 7 minutes. Before serving, season with salt and pepper.

Serves 6

creamy coleslaw

see variations page 257

Coleslaw has been a popular side dish since the days of ancient Rome. This version is especially appealing because the red cabbage lifts the otherwise muted colours.

235 ml (8 fl oz) mayonnaise
3 tbsp granulated sugar
2 tbsp white wine vinegar
5 tbsp vegetable oil
$1/4$ tsp onion granules
$1/4$ tsp dry mustard
$1/4$ tsp celery salt
1 tbsp fresh lemon juice

120 ml (4 fl oz) whipping cream
Sea salt and freshly ground black pepper
500 g (1 lb 2 oz) green cabbage, finely
    shredded
55 g (2 oz) red cabbage, finely shredded
$1/2$ small onion, peeled and chopped
1 celery stick, thinly sliced
1 carrot, grated

Blend together the mayonnaise, sugar, vinegar and oil. Add the onion granules, dry mustard, celery salt, lemon juice, cream, salt and pepper. Stir until smooth. Pour the coleslaw dressing over the shredded cabbage, onion, celery and carrot in a large bowl. Toss until the vegetables are well coated and chill until ready to serve.

Serves 6

variations

potato salad with cucumber and dill

see base recipe page 231

new potato salad with ham
Use new potatoes in place of red-skinned potatoes. Replace the cucumber, spring onions, dill and dressing with a mixture of 120 ml (4 fl oz) vegetable oil; 60 ml (2 fl oz) each of cider vinegar, Creole mustard and Dijon mustard; 2 tablespoons Worcestershire sauce; ½ teaspoon cayenne pepper; and 85 g (3 oz) each of chopped ham, diced onion and chopped celery.

blue cheese and walnut potato salad
Instead of the cucumber, spring onions, dill and dressing, mix the following into the salad bowl: 55 g (2 oz) toasted chopped walnuts; 4 tablespoons each of milk, finely chopped fresh parsley and crumbled blue cheese; 235 ml (8 fl oz) soured cream; 1 tablespoon granulated sugar; and ½ teaspoon dry mustard.

sicilian potato salad
Instead of the cucumber, dressing and dill, mix the following into the salad: 4 tablespoons each of red wine vinegar, chopped flat-leaf parsley, chopped black olives and drained capers; 200 ml (7 fl oz) extra-virgin olive oil; 2 tablespoons chopped fresh oregano; 1 tablespoon each of chopped anchovies and crushed garlic; and a pinch crushed dried chillies.

potato salad with spicy cheese dressing
Replace the dressing, dill and cucumber with 5 cooked and crumbled bacon rashers, 175 ml (6 fl oz) cream cheese dip, 1 tablespoon hot sauce, 85 g (3 oz) each of sliced spring onions and sweet pickle relish, and ¼ green pepper, chopped.

variations

picnic-style potato salad

see base recipe page 232

american potato salad with hard-boiled eggs and sweet pickles
Replace the celery, diced cucumber and spring onion with 2 tablespoons chopped
fresh parsley.

jalapeño potato salad
Replace the dressing with the following, whisked together: 120 ml (4 fl oz) extra-virgin olive
oil and 2 tablespoons each of mayonnaise and Dijon mustard. Mix into the salad
4 tablespoons each of sliced spring onions and crumbled feta cheese, 2 seeded and finely
chopped fresh chillies, 2 tablespoons white wine vinegar and 2 crushed cloves garlic.

sweet potato–apple salad
Replace the potatoes with 1.35 kg (3 lbs) sweet potatoes. Omit the celery, cucumber and
spring onions. Instead of the picnic-style dressing, mix the potatoes with 1 apple, cored and
diced; 55 g (2 oz) chopped pecans; 60 ml (2 fl oz) each of soured cream and mayonnaise;
1 teaspoon grated lemon zest; 2 tablespoons each of fresh lemon juice and honey and
¼ teaspoon dried tarragon.

jamaican potato salad
Omit the diced cucumber. Replace with 4 thick streaky bacon rashers, cooked and crumbled;
285 ml (10 fl oz) mayonnaise; 1 tablespoon each of dry mustard and fresh thyme; ½ teaspoon
each of ground allspice and turmeric; pinch of cayenne pepper; 6 diced cornichons;
4 tablespoons each of chopped celery and onion; and 2 teaspoons hot sauce.

variations

barbecued corn on the cob

see base recipe page 235

barbecued corn italian-style
Replace the butter, chilli powder, onion, salt and pepper with a mixture of 60 ml (2 fl oz) olive oil, 1 teaspoon Italian seasoning, and sea salt and cracked black pepper to taste.

corn on the cob with spicy lime butter
Omit the butter, chilli powder, salt and pepper. Make a flavoured butter to serve with the corn: blend together 45 g (4 oz) softened unsalted butter, grated zest of 1 lime, 1 chopped fresh red chilli and salt to taste. Chill. Grill corn as in the base recipe, serving a disc of the butter on top of each grilled ear so that it melts into the corn.

cajun-grilled corn on the cob
Prepare the base recipe. Roll the grilled corn in a rub made from 1 teaspoon each of dried oregano and paprika; $3/4$ teaspoon each of crushed clove garlic and onion granules; $1/2$ teaspoon salt; $1/4$ teaspoon dried thyme and black pepper and $1/8$ teaspoon cayenne.

corn on the cob with red wine butter
Prepare the corn as in the base recipe but do not wrap the cobs in foil. Baste the corn while grilling with a mixture of 70 g ($2^{1}/_{2}$ oz) melted butter and 120 ml (4 fl oz) red wine.

cumin grilled corn
Replace the chilli powder and onion salt with $1^{1}/_{2}$ teaspoons ground cumin, $1/2$ teaspoon salt and $1/2$ teaspoon turmeric. Proceed with the base recipe.

variations

spanish coleslaw

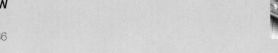

see base recipe page 236

cabbage and corn slaw
Omit the celery salt and dry mustard. Add to the base recipe 340 g (12 oz) sweetcorn,
1 finely chopped red onion, ¼ seeded and chopped yellow pepper, 1 to 2 tablespoons seeded
and chopped fresh red chilli pepper, 4 tablespoons granulated sugar, 5 tablespoons each of
white vinegar and vegetable oil and ½ teaspoon freshly ground black pepper.

sweet and sassy vanilla slaw
Replace the green cabbage with Chinese leaves. In place of the peppers, use 225 g (8 oz)
each of chopped raw broccoli stems and peeled and grated carrot. Omit the mustard
and celery salt from the dressing and replace them with 85 g (3 oz) granulated sugar,
2 teaspoons vanilla extract, ½ teaspoon ground ginger and ¼ teaspoon cayenne.

mango slaw
Replace the cabbage and peppers with 1 mango and 1 red pepper, both peeled and cut into
julienne, and 1 large fresh red chilli pepper, seeded and chopped. Omit the celery salt, vinegar
and mustard from the dressing and replace them with the juice of 2 limes and 2 tablespoons
each of fresh chopped coriander and parsley.

carolina slaw
Replace the peppers with ½ small onion, finely chopped and 2 grated carrots. In place
of the dressing, in a saucepan mix 85 g (3 oz) granulated sugar, 1 teaspoon salt, 80 ml
(2½ fl oz) vegetable oil, 1 teaspoon celery seeds and 160 ml (5 fl oz) cider vinegar. Bring to
the boil, leave to cool and pour over vegetables.

variations

garlic bread

see base recipe page 239

parsley-garlic bread
Replace the oregano and dill with 2 additional tablespoons dried parsley and ¼ teaspoon paprika (optional).

mozzarella-garlic bread
Replace the parsley, oregano, dill and Parmesan with 1 teaspoon Worcestershire sauce and 225 g (8 oz) mozzarella cheese, coarsely grated.

most delicious garlic-cheese bread
Replace the butter, parsley, oregano and dill with a mixture of 4 tablespoons olive oil, 2 additional crushed large cloves garlic, 175 ml (6 fl oz) mayonnaise and 150 g (5½ oz) freshly grated Parmesan. Omit the Parmesan cheese sprinkled on top in the base recipe.

go-go garlic bread
Replace the dill with 120 ml (4 fl oz) mayonnaise, 1 tablespoon grated Parmesan, ¼ teaspoon dried basil, ¼ teaspoon seasoning salt and 55 g (2 oz) grated Cheddar cheese.

gremolata garlic bread
Replace the oregano and dill with 1½ teaspoons grated lemon zest. Increase the quantity of dried parsley in the flavoured butter to 2 teaspoons.

scalloped green beans

see base recipe page 240

green bean casserole
Replace the cheese sauce with a 300 g (10½ oz) tin condensed cream of mushroom soup. Top the finished casserole with 150 g (5½ oz) dried onions instead of the breadcrumbs.

creamy green bean casserole
Replace the cheese sauce with a sauce made of 225 g (8 oz) cream cheese at room temperature, 120 ml (4 fl oz) milk, 2 tablespoons ranch-style salad dressing, ¼ teaspoon white pepper, 1 chopped onion, 2 crushed cloves garlic, 85 g (3 oz) sliced fresh mushrooms and 40 g (1½ oz) fresh breadcrumbs.

holiday green beans
Replace the cheese sauce with a mixture of 4 tablespoons each of double cream, chopped mushrooms, toasted walnuts and coarsely chopped spring onions; add garlic salt to taste. Instead of the breadcrumbs, top with 4 bacon rashers, cooked and crumbled.

green bean casserole with tomatoes and mozzarella
Replace the cheese sauce with a mixture of 2 plum tomatoes, seeded and diced; 225 g (8 oz) grated mozzarella; ½ onion, finely chopped; and 120 ml (4 fl oz) each of double cream and soured cream. Instead of the breadcrumbs, top with a 28 g (1 oz) packet of crushed soured cream and chive crisps.

variations

baked beans

see base recipe page 243

apple baked beans
Replace the bacon, sugar, onion, pepper and barbecue sauce with 235 ml (8 fl oz) apple juice;
1 teaspoon salt, 1 teaspoon dry mustard, 225 g (8 oz) cooked and chopped bacon, 120 ml
(4 fl oz) black treacle, 2 chopped celery sticks and 2 crisp apples, peeled, cored and chopped.

peachy baked beans
Replace the bacon and pepper with a 400 g (14 oz) can peaches, drained and chopped,
1 large red pepper, seeded and sliced, 1 teaspoon sea salt and freshly ground black
pepper to taste.

pineapple-bourbon baked beans
Replace the bacon, sugar, onion, pepper and barbecue sauce with 1 teaspoon dry mustard;
2 tablespoons chilli sauce; 225 g (8 oz) can crushed pineapple, drained; 2 tablespoons black
treacle; 4 tablespoons good-quality bourbon and ½ cup strong coffee.

cola baked beans
Replace the bacon, onion, pepper, sugar and barbecue sauce with a 350 g (12 oz) can cola.

cherry cola baked beans
Replace the bacon, onion, pepper, sugar and barbecue sauce with a 350 g (12 oz) can cherry
cola. Add 55 g (2 oz) stoned cherries to the beans.

caribbean pinto beans

see base recipe page 244

beans and greens
Replace the pepper, barbecued meat and sauce with 455 g (1 lb) each of sliced smoked sausage and shredded spring greens and add 1 teaspoon crushed chillies. Proceed with the base recipe.

hard rock café barbecued beans
Replace the vegetables, oil, meat, flavourings and sauce with 2 tablespoons water, 2 tablespoons cornflour, 120 ml (4 fl oz) ketchup, 4 tablespoons each of white vinegar and light brown sugar, 2 tablespoons chopped onion, 1 teaspoon prepared mustard, ½ teaspoon chilli powder, ¼ teaspoon each of salt and freshly ground black pepper and 85 g (3 oz) cooked bacon. Proceed with the base recipe.

barbecued cowboy pinto beans
Replace the pepper and barbecued meat with 1 tablespoon chilli powder, 120 ml (4 fl oz) ketchup, 2 tablespoons prepared yellow mustard and a dash of Tabasco sauce. Proceed with the base recipe.

el paso border beans
Replace the pepper, meat and sauce with 2 tablespoons lard or vegetable oil; 5 bacon rashers, cooked and chopped; 115 g (4 oz) cooked and chopped chorizo; 455 g (1 lb) tomatoes, peeled, seeded and chopped; 6 mild red chillies, seeded and chopped; and 1 teaspoon ground cumin. Proceed with the base recipe.

variations

garlic and dill grilled potatoes

see base recipe page 246

baked potatoes on the grill
Replace the onions, cheese, garlic, butter and dill with 5 tablespoons melted unsalted butter, 4 thinly sliced spring onions and 85 g (3 oz) sliced button mushrooms.

roasted potato parcels
Replace the cheese, garlic, butter and dill with 1 green pepper, seeded and cut into strips; 4 tablespoons olive oil; 4 tablespoons balsamic vinegar and lemon pepper to taste.

grilled potato and onion parcels
Replace the cheese, garlic, butter and dill with 150 ml (5 fl oz) olive oil; 1 tablespoon Dijon mustard; 2 tablespoons chopped fresh thyme and 2 large red onions, halved and sliced 1.5 cm (½ in) thick. Garnish cooked potatoes with fresh thyme sprigs.

grilled garlic potatoes with corn
Replace the onions, cheese, garlic and dill with 340 g (12 oz) sweetcorn. Make a dressing by whisking together 6 roasted large garlic cloves; 4 tablespoons olive oil; 1 tablespoon each of finely chopped fresh rosemary, white wine vinegar and Dijon mustard; and 2 thinly sliced spring onions.

variations

creamy coleslaw

see base recipe page 247

southern coleslaw
Replace the red cabbage and the dressing with 1 red pepper, seeded and chopped, 1 teaspoon celery seeds and 4 tablespoons mayonnaise, and mix. Place 235 ml (8 fl oz) water, 3 tablespoons white vinegar and 2 tablespoons granulated sugar into a saucepan. Bring to the boil and pour over the coleslaw.

honey deli-style coleslaw
Omit the red cabbage. Replace the dressing with the following ingredients, stirred together to blend: 120 ml (4 fl oz) honey, 1 teaspoon celery seeds and 120 ml (4 fl oz) each of soured cream and mayonnaise.

coleslaw with creamy tangy dressing
Omit the red cabbage. Replace the dressing with the following ingredients, stirred together: 285 ml (10 fl oz) mayonnaise, 85 g (3 oz) granulated sugar, 60 ml (2 fl oz) white wine vinegar and ¼ teaspoon celery seeds.

cabbage slaw with apple and raisins
Replace the red cabbage and onion with 4 unpeeled, cored and diced apples and 85 g (3 oz) raisins. Omit the dressing and replace with 355 ml (12 fl oz) low-fat mayonnaise.

sweet sizzlers

A surprising range of sweet treats can be cooked up on a grill, and this chapter shows you how. It also contains desserts prepared in other ways, which are great to serve at the end of a barbecue to round things off in style.

peach cobbler

see variations page 273

Especially good topped with a scoop of homemade vanilla ice cream, this is a wonderful way to finish a barbecue supper.

6 peaches, peeled and sliced
100 g (3½ oz) granulated sugar
2 tbsp fresh lemon juice
1 tsp pure vanilla
½ tsp ground ginger
¼ tsp freshly grated nutmeg
155 g (5 oz) plain flour

55 g (2 oz) caster sugar
1½ tsp baking powder
½ tsp bicarbonate of soda
¼ tsp salt
55 g (2 oz) unsalted butter, chilled and cubed
150 ml (5 fl oz) buttermilk
Additional granulated sugar to sprinkle on top

Combine the first 6 ingredients. Spoon the peach mixture into a greased, large shallow baking dish. Cover with foil and bake at 200°C (400°F / Gas mark 5) for 15 minutes or until the peach mixture is hot and bubbly.

Meanwhile, to prepare the biscuit topping, combine the flour, caster sugar, baking powder, bicarbonate of soda and salt in a bowl. Cut in the butter with a pastry knife until the mixture resembles coarse crumbs. Add the buttermilk and stir just until combined. Remove the dish from the oven and uncover. Drop large spoonfuls of the dough evenly on top of the peach mixture. Lightly sprinkle additional sugar over the dough. Continue baking, uncovered, for 30 minutes or until the scones are golden and a skewer inserted in the centre of the scones comes out clean. Serve warm with cream or ice cream.

Serves 4

summer fruit parcels

see variations page 274

Fresh mint adds a wonderful depth of flavour to fruit, especially when the flavour is enhanced with sugar and citrus. Next time you make a fruit salad, add some finely chopped fresh mint for a little extra zing.

2 peaches
Boiling water
225 g (8 oz) strawberries, hulled and washed
225 g (8 oz) cherries, pitted
2 kiwifruit, peeled and sliced

55g (2 oz) unsalted butter
2 tbsp light brown sugar
Grated zest and juice of 1 orange
4 sprigs fresh mint

Place the peaches in a bowl and pour boiling water over them. Let stand for 1 minute, then drain and peel. Cut the peaches in half, remove their stones, and slice. Put the cherries and strawberries in a large bowl and add the sliced peaches and kiwifruit. Gently mix.

Cut 4 large squares of heavy-duty foil. Divide the fruit between the squares. Heat the butter, sugar, orange zest, and orange juice over a medium heat in a small saucepan until the sugar has melted. Spoon this mixture over the fruit and top each portion with a sprig of mint. Close the parcels, being sure to secure the seams.

Grill the parcels over a medium heat for about 10 minutes. Serve with whipped cream or ice cream.

Serves 4

texas sheet cake with chocolate frosting

see variations page 275

This rich cake with its sumptuously sweet frosting is an American classic.

One 500 g (1 lb 2 oz) packet chocolate cake mix
235 ml (8 fl oz) buttermilk
70 g (2½ oz) unsalted butter, melted
2 large eggs, lightly beaten
1 tsp vanilla essence
for chocolate frosting
6 tbsp milk

4 tbsp cocoa powder
115 g (4 oz) butter, softened
455 g (1 lb) icing sugar, sifted
1 tsp vanilla essence
115 g (4 oz) toasted chopped pecan nuts

Beat together the first 5 ingredients with an electric mixer at full speed for 2 minutes or until blended. Pour into a greased and floured 33 x 23 x 5 cm (13 x 9 x 2 in) baking tin. Bake at 180°C (350°F) for 15 to 20 minutes or until a wooden skewer inserted in the middle comes out clean.

Meanwhile, prepare the frosting. Start by mixing the milk and cocoa powder in a heavy-based saucepan. Add the butter and, over a medium heat, stir until it melts. Remove from the heat and gradually stir in the icing sugar and vanilla essence until smooth. Add the pecans.

When the cake is just out of the oven, spread the frosting evenly over the hot cake. Let it cool before serving.

Serves 6

grandma's fried fruit pies

see variations page 276

No fruit pie will ever taste as good as my grandma's. Luckily she left me the recipe so I can pass it on to you.

340 g (12 oz) plain flour
1 tsp salt
170 g (6 oz) vegetable shortening
1 egg, lightly beaten
4 tbsp cold water
1 tsp white wine vinegar
1½ 400 g (14 oz) cans apple pie filling

Mix together the flour and salt. Cut in the shortening with a fork until the mixture resembles coarse crumbs. Stir together the beaten egg and the water, and sprinkle over the flour mixture. Sprinkle in the vinegar and mix lightly, until the ingredients are well combined. Form the dough into a ball and wrap in clingfilm. Refrigerate for at least one hour.

Roll out the dough thinly. Cut into 7.5 cm (3 in) rounds. Divide the filling between the rounds, piling it up in the middle of the pastry. Fold over the rounds, damp the edges, then press together to form semi-circles. Let the pies stand for a few minutes before frying.

There are two methods of frying: deep-fry, at 190°C (375°F) for 3 to 4 minutes; or pan-fry the pies in about 1.5 cm (½ in) of oil in an electric frying pan set to 190°C (375°F) for 5 to 6 minutes. In both cases, fry in the hot vegetable oil until golden brown. Remove from the fat and drain. Sprinkle the hot pies with icing sugar or cinnamon sugar.

Serves 6–8

grilled s'mores

see variations page 277

This version of North America's favourite fireside treat will be a sure-fire hit with children at the end of a barbecue party.

flour tortillas
1 jar peanut butter
1 bag miniature chocolate chips
1 bag miniature marshmallows

Spread peanut butter on half of the tortilla shells. Sprinkle with chocolate chips and marshmallows. Grill the plain and filled tortillas at the same time, for about 3 to 4 minutes. Flip a plain tortilla on top of each filled one. Cut into wedges and serve.

Alternatively, you could roll the filled tortillas up like a burrito and wrap each one in heavy-duty foil. Seal the ends by folding over the foil. Place on the edge of the fire or above the coals until heated through, then unwrap and enjoy.

Serves 4–6

grilled pineapple with syrup-lime butter

see variations page 278

This sweet butter is the perfect partner for soft, ripe pineapple slices.

1 ripe pineapple, peeled and cored, top and
    bottom removed
Vegetable oil
Salt and freshly ground black pepper to taste

4 tablespoons golden syrup
55 g (2 oz) butter
2 tbsp fresh lime juice

Cut the pineapple across into 6 slices, each about 2.5 cm (1 in) thick. Brush the cut surfaces of the pineapple slices lightly with oil; sprinkle with salt and pepper. Grill over medium heat for about 8 to 10 minutes, until golden brown. Turn and grill the other side to brown it. Meanwhile, combine the syrup, butter and lime juice in a small saucepan, and stir together over a low heat until the butter is melted. Remove the pineapple slices from the grill, brush with syrup-lime butter and serve.

Serves 6

glazed pears

see variations page 279

Spooning a wine-based syrup over pears before grilling makes the fruit taste delectable.

6 large pears
Grated zest and juice of ½ lemon
4 tbsp maple syrup
1 tsp vanilla essence
4 tbsp red wine
3 tbsp chopped pistachio nuts

Peel, core and halve the pears. Cut 6 squares of heavy-duty foil and lay a halved pear on each piece of foil. Combine the remaining ingredients except the pistachios in a small saucepan and heat to boiling point. Remove from the heat and spoon the mixture over each pear. Close the foil parcels, being sure to secure the seams.

Grill the pears for 5 to 8 minutes over a medium heat, until they are hot and tender but retain their shape. Open each parcel and brush or spoon the juices from the parcel back over the fruit. Sprinkle a few chopped pistachio nuts over each portion and serve.

Serves 6

peaches with blue cheese and honey

see variations page 280

Blue cheese isn't often used in desserts – but its rich creaminess is essential here.

6 ripe peaches, halved and pitted
2 tbsp vegetable oil
4 tbsp blue cheese or mascarpone
4 tbsp clear honey

Black pepper to taste
Fresh mint leaves or sprigs for garnish

Brush the cut sides of the peaches with oil and place on a grill preheated to medium, cut-side down. Grill until caramelized. Turn over and grill until almost soft, about 1 to 2 minutes more.

Transfer the peaches to a platter, cut-sides up, and place a spoonful of cheese in the centre of each. Drizzle with honey and grind fresh pepper to taste over the peaches. Garnish with mint and serve.

Serves 6

homemade vanilla ice cream

see variations page 281

No shop-bought ice cream tastes as good as homemade; and this version is particularly appealing, without any tricky custard-making or constant stirring.

1 l (1³/₄ pt) single cream
400 g (14 oz) can sweetened condensed milk
100 g (3¹/₂ oz) caster sugar
3 tsp vanilla essence

475 ml (16 fl oz) whipping cream (for
   refrigerator-freezer method only)

In a large ice cream maker container, combine all the ingredients and mix well. Freeze according to the manufacturer's instructions; this should take about 40 minutes.

Alternatively, try the refrigerator-freezer method. Omit the single cream. In a large bowl, combine the sweetened condensed milk and vanilla. Fold in 475 ml (16 fl oz) whipping cream, whipped. Pour into a 23 x 13 cm (9 x 5 in) loaf tin or another large container. Cover and freeze for 6 hours or until firm.

Serves 4–6

variations

peach cobbler

see base recipe page 259

blueberry cobbler
Replace the peaches and lemon juice with 680 g (1½ lbs) blueberries, 100 g (3½ oz) caster sugar and 75 ml (2½ fl oz) water. Use 1 tablespoon ground cinnamon in place of the ginger.

peach-berry cobbler
Reduce the number of peaches to 3. Omit the lemon juice and ginger. Add 400 g (14 oz) berries and 280 g (10 oz) additional sugar.

blackberry cobbler
Replace the peaches and lemon juice with 680 g (1½ lbs) blackberries, 255 g (9 oz) caster sugar, 3 tablespoons cornflour and 2 tablespoons unsalted butter.

sour cherry cobbler
Replace the peaches and ginger with 400 g (14 oz) stoned morello cherries, 120 ml (4 fl oz) water, 140 g (5 oz) caster sugar and 1 tablespoon cornflour.

variations

summer fruit parcels

see base recipe page 260

summer fruit parcels with kirsch
Prepare the basic recipe, adding 1 tablespoon kirsch to each parcel.

fruits of the forest parcels
Prepare the basic recipe, replacing the peaches and kiwifruit with 225 g (8 oz) raspberries and the same quantity of blueberries.

tropical fruit parcels
Prepare the basic recipe, replacing the peaches, strawberries and cherries with 225 g (8 oz) pineapple chunks and 225 g (8 oz) papaya chunks.

summer fruit parcels with white wine
Prepare the basic recipe, adding 1 tablespoon white wine to each parcel.

texas sheet cake with chocolate frosting

see base recipe page 263

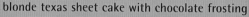

blonde texas sheet cake with chocolate frosting
Replace the chocolate cake mix with white chocolate cake mix.

lazy daisy sheet cake with buttermilk frosting
Make the cake as in the base recipe. Replace the frosting with 150 ml (5 fl oz) light brown sugar and 3 tablespoons buttermilk, combined in a bowl. Garnish with 150 ml (5 fl oz) toasted chopped pecans.

carrot sheet cake with cream cheese frosting
Replace the chocolate cake mix with a carrot cake mix. Make a cream cheese frosting by combining 55g (2 oz) softened butter; 310 g (11 oz) cream cheese, softened; and ½ teaspoon vanilla essence.

chocolate sheet cake with chocolate coconut frosting
Prepare the frosting as in the base recipe, adding 125 g (4½ oz) toasted shredded coconut to the ingredients.

variations

grandma's fried fruit pies

see base recipe page 264

peach fried pies
Prepare the basic recipe, replacing the apple pie filling with 700 g (1½ lbs) tinned peaches.

black cherry fried pies
Prepare the basic recipe, replacing the apple pie filling with 700 g (1½ lbs) tinned stoned black cherries.

blueberry fried pies
Prepare the basic recipe, replacing the apple pie filling with 700 g (1½ lbs) blueberries.

french apple fried pies
Prepare the basic recipe and add 2 tablespoons each of sultanas and currants, 1 teaspoon ground cinnamon and 1 teaspoon grated lemon zest to the apple pie filling.

dried fruit fried pies
Prepare the basic recipe, replacing the apple pie filling with 500 g (1 lb 2 oz) mixed dried fruit such as apples, apricots, pears and peaches.

grilled s'mores

see base recipe page 267

fluffy nutters
Replace the chocolate chips and marshmallows with a 225 g (8 oz) jar marshmallow fluff.

open-faced cinnamon crisp
Replace the peanut butter, chocolate chips and marshmallows with a cinnamon filling, made by combining 225 g (8 oz) melted butter, 55 g (2 oz) granulated sugar, and 1 tablespoon ground cinnamon. Do not place an unfilled tortilla over the top of each filled one.

open-faced mascarpone gorgonzola torte
Replace the peanut butter, chocolate chips and marshmallows with 225 g (8 oz) mascarpone, 115 g (4 oz) crumbled gorgonzola and 85 g (3 oz) blueberries. Do not place an unfilled tortilla over the top of each filled one.

snickers delight dessert tortillas
Replace the peanut butter, marshmallows and chocolate chips with 115 g (4 oz) bar chocolate with almonds; 3 large Snickers chocolate bars, chopped up; and 115 g (4 oz) sweetened desiccated coconut.

variations

grilled pineapple with syrup-lime butter

see base recipe page 268

honeysuckle pineapple

Prepare the basic recipe, replacing the syrup, butter and lime juice with a mixture of
60 ml (2 fl oz) honey, 2 tablespoons cherry brandy and 1 tablespoon fresh lemon juice.

grilled sweet curried pineapple

Omit the syrup, butter and lime juice. Instead rub the pineapple before grilling with a
mixture of 55 g (2 oz) packed dark brown sugar and 1/2 teaspoon curry powder or to taste.
Grill the pineapple as in the base recipe. Pour 120 ml (4 fl oz) plain yoghurt over the grilled
pineapple and garnish with 3 tablespoons toasted desiccated coconut.

grilled piña colada

Omit the syrup, butter and lime juice. Grill the pineapple as in the base recipe. Pour a sauce
made by combining 60 ml (2 fl oz) tinned coconut milk, 1 tablespoon light rum, 55 g (2 oz)
granulated sugar and 1 tablespoon ground cinnamon over the grilled fruit.

hot buttered rum pineapple

Omit the syrup and lime. Instead, flavour the melted butter with 55 g (2 oz) brown sugar,
2 tablespoons dark rum, 1 tablespoon ground cinnamon and 1/2 teaspoon each of ground
ginger, nutmeg and cloves. Grill the pineapple as in the base recipe.

variations

glazed pears

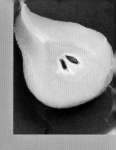

see base recipe page 269

glazed pears with white wine syrup
Prepare the base recipe, replacing the red wine with white wine.

glazed pears with brandy syrup
Prepare the base recipe, replacing the red wine with brandy.

glazed pears with chocolate sauce
Prepare the base recipe, replacing the red wine with 55 g (2 oz) chocolate chips, divided equally among the 6 foil parcels.

moroccan-style glazed pears
Prepare the base recipe, omitting the wine and adding 2 drops orange-flower water and 2 drops rosewater to each packet.

variations

peaches with blue cheese and honey

see base recipe page 270

grilled peaches and cream
Replace the cheese and pepper with 2 tablespoons honey and 225 g (8 oz) cream cheese.

sweet grilled glazed peaches
Replace the cheese and pepper with 120 ml (4 fl oz) honey and 2 tablespoons ground cinnamon.

grilled peaches with raspberry puree
Omit the cheese, honey and pepper. Barbecue the peaches as in the base recipe, basting regularly with a glaze made by mixing 2 tablespoons brown sugar, $1/4$ teaspoon ground cinnamon, 2 teaspoons dark rum and 2 teaspoons melted unsalted butter. Serve the grilled peaches with a sauce made by combining 120 ml (4 fl oz) seedless raspberry jam and 2 teaspoons of fresh lemon juice.

grilled balsamic-glazed peaches
Omit the cheese and honey. Spread a glaze made by mixing 120 ml (4 fl oz) balsamic vinegar and 3 tablespoons light brown sugar over the peach halves. Proceed to barbecue as in the base recipe.

variations

homemade vanilla ice cream

see base recipe page 272

peach ice cream
Omit 2 teaspoons of the vanilla essence. Prepare the ice cream as in the base recipe,
flavouring it by stirring in 475 ml (16 fl oz) mashed peaches, 1 teaspoon almond essence and
a few drops each of yellow and red food colouring before freezing.

strawberry ice cream
Omit 2 teaspoons of the vanilla essence. Prepare the ice cream as in the base recipe,
flavouring it by stirring in 475 ml (16 fl oz) mashed strawberries and a few drops of red food
colouring before freezing.

banana ice cream
Omit 2 teaspoons of the vanilla essence. Prepare the ice cream as in the base recipe, mashing
4 ripe medium bananas and stirring them into the ice cream before freezing.

chocolate ice cream
Prepare the ice cream as in the base recipe, replacing the sugar, single cream and vanilla
essence with 150 ml (5 fl oz) chocolate sauce and 475 ml (16 fl oz) double cream.

index